ARIZONA'S NATURAL ENVIRONMENT

ARIZONA'S NATURAL ENVIRONMENT

Landscapes and Habitats

CHARLES H. LOWE

THE UNIVERSITY OF ARIZONA PRESS
Tucson, Arizona

Third printing 1977

THE UNIVERSITY OF ARIZONA PRESS

From *The Vertebrates of Arizona*
Copyright © 1964
The Arizona Board of Regents
All Rights Reserved
Manufactured in the U.S.A.

I. S. B. N.-0-8165-0349-4

CONTENTS

FIGURES

(Photographs are by the authors unless otherwise credited)

TABLES

ARIZONA LANDSCAPES AND HABITATS

INTRODUCTION

The variety and beauty of the landscapes of Arizona have been remarked upon by naturalists who have long-traveled to this remarkable state from many parts of the World. This introduction to the Arizona vertebrate animal check lists provides an illustrated account of these natural settings for the homes of animals and plants in the state, and a discussion of the systems employed by biologists to classify them. Some references are given to aid those interested in further exploration of the subject.

Arizona is not only a desert. It is one of the most topographically varied and scenic areas in North America and contains extensive forests occurring up to timberline elevations (11,000-11,400 feet) plus a bit of alpine tundra above timberline on the summit of San Francisco Mountain (to 12,670 feet). This great environmental diversity is reflected in Arizona's diverse fauna in which there is a total of 64 species of fishes, 22 species of amphibians, 94 species of reptiles, 434 species of birds, and 137 species of mammals, a combined total of 751 species which does not include several others listed as "hypothetical" for Arizona.[1]

Habitats

The vertebrates occupy the two major kinds of habitats, those on land and those in water. The general term *habitat* refers to the natural environs of a species of plant or animal — the place where it lives and makes its living. Habitats may be small (microhabitats) or large (macrohabitats). The latter may be large community habitats where many species of plants and animals live — the habitats of biotic communities — and each species occupies its own ecologic niche within the community.

Habitats themselves, just as plants and animals, reveal certain similarities and differences. Because of this, a check list of habitats can be arranged (Table 1) that is similar to a check list of animals, say of birds. Thus, in addition to the *taxonomic classification* (*systematic hierarchy*) for animals and plants (*e.g.*, species, genus, family, order, etc.) which is based on phylogeny and heredity,[2] there is an *ecologic classification* (*e.g.*,

---

[1] Numbers are based on the check lists of this series (1964).

[2] See Mayr, Linsley, and Usinger (1953) for principles and procedures in classification. Recent symposia entitled "The Species Problem" (Mayr, 1957), "Species: Modern Concepts" (Lewis, Maslin, Durrant, Phillips, Lowe, 1959), and "Vertebrate Speciation" (Blair, 1961) contain papers by western naturalists which treat species problems in Arizona and other southwestern states, in addition to the general problem of the mechanisms in the formation of species.

association, association-type, formation, formation-class, etc.) based primarily on life-form and environment, for example as follows:[3]

> *Woodland* Formation-class
>   *Evergreen Woodland* Formation
>   *Oak Woodland* (*Quercus*) Association-type
>   *Emory oak-Arizona oak* Association

While ecologic classification is natural, it lacks the unifying theme of phylogenetic relationship that is found in taxonomic classification. Of course, natural landscapes do evolve and have evolutionary relationships of their own. The story of the evolution of vegetation, *e.g.*, of our forests, grasslands, deserts, etc., is one of the most fascinating stories in ecology and evolution (see Chaney, Dorf, and Axelrod, 1944; Axelrod, 1950, 1958; Deevey, 1949; Dorf, 1960; Martin, Schoenwetter and Arms, 1961). Moreover, it is obvious that *natural selection* (Darwin, 1859) is an ecological concept.

Plants have left relatively abundant fossil remains (as compared to animals) and these are frequently in the form of leaves (megafossils) and pollen (microfossils). This has proved important to modern paleoecologic investigation of the evolution of biotic communities. For example, investigation by the floristic method which aids reconstruction of past environments by comparison of a fossil flora with the living vegetation which resembles it most closely (see references cited above for Chaney, *et al.*, and Axelrod). Norris (1958), Gray (1961), and Martin and Gray (1962) have recently analyzed Pleistocene events in the arid Southwest and events in the West during late Tertiary. Darrow (1961) has recently discussed the origin and development of the vegetational communities of the Southwest, and Turner (1959) also reviewed Axelrod's work with special reference to this area.

Why is the ecologic classification of terrestrial biotic communities based essentially on plants? The answer is not hard to appreciate. Plants, in their varied forms and quantitative relationships, constitute one of the essential features of landscape, and hence of landscape classification. The plants are always out there "taking it" — for 24 hours a day for all 365 days of the year. They continuously respond by species, numbers, sizes, sites, etc. to the factors controlling the biotic (plant-animal) community. Thus they most faithfully express the *effective environment* to the observer. Animals are more or less secretive by day or by night, and often indeed for one or more entire seasons. There is no question that the vegetation

---

[3] This is a conventional form of ecologic classification. See Fosberg (1961) for a different scheme.

The smallest possible unit in such an ecological classification, the ecological niche, is not included here. Each species within the "association" occupies its own peculiar ecologic niche ("address" + "occupation") in the biotic community.

offers for the present the most satisfactory basis for the recognition and classification of the major terrestrial communities.

It is the *native perennial plants* that are the ever-present, sensitive, readily observed, measureable and mappable indicators of the environmental controls, which are climate, soil, topography, and biotic factors including man, his domestics, and man-made fire.[4] The perennials constitute the important fraction of the plant-animal community that we perceive as vegetation and classify in any meaningful hierarchy of natural communities. In short, as vegetation, native perennial plants are the classifiable and mappable indicators of the environments also inhabited by the animals; hence by the entire biotic community.

Thus, by and large, it is the plants rather than the animals that tell us more precisely what the overall environmental conditions were at a given place and time in the geological yesterday, as well as what the effective environments are in a given area today.

The following illustrated references are available and particularly useful for aid in recognizing native plants in Arizona: Benson (1940), Benson and Darrow (1944), Preston (1947), Little (1950), Gould (1951), Humphrey, Brown, and Everson (1956). Kearney and Peebles' (1942, 1951, 1960) flora for Arizona is a more extensive work; the more comprehensive flora for California (Munz and Keck, 1959), which includes a large number of species common to both states, is more recent and considerably better from an evolutionary point of view (*Larrea divaricata* for creosotebush, *Cereus giganteus* for sahuaro, etc).[5] Little's (1953) checklist is the most recent available for trees. Standard and illustrated works on North American trees are Martinez (1945, 1948) for pines, Sargent's (1926) manual, Sudworth's (1915 to 1934) series of papers on species of the Rocky Mountain region, and Munn's (1938) maps. The popular series on flowers published by the Southwest Monuments Association are useful (Dodge, 1958; Arnberger, 1957; Patraw, 1953).

Pearson's (1931 and elsewhere) and Shreve's (1942a and elsewhere) accounts of the vegetation of Arizona are excellent, and Nichol's (1937, 1952) vegetation map is still serviceable after 25 years (although in need of revision) as are the map and the classifications on which it was based (Shreve, 1917; Livingston and Shreve, 1921; Shantz and Zon, 1924; Shantz, 1936; and others). Humphrey's (1950, 1953, 1955, 1960) illustrated papers with maps of Arizona grassland vegetation are available for many counties; Darrow (1944), for Cochise County. Other maps

---

[4] For discussions of fire and Arizona vegetation, see Leopold (1924), Pearson (1931), Humphrey (1949, 1951, 1958, 1962), Reynolds and Bohning (1956), Marshall (1957, 1962), and Cooper (1960, 1961b).

[5] The scientific names for plants used here may be found (with few exceptions) in the following works which, of course, are not always in agreement: Little (1953), Benson (1940), Benson and Darrow (1944, 1954), Munz and Keck (1959), Kearney and Peebles (1951, 1960).

covering parts of Arizona are provided by Bryan, 1925; Baker, 1945; U. S. Forest Service, 1949; Marshall, 1957; Martin, *et al.*, 1961; and others (see Melton, 1959, for a map series illustrating a geomorphic history of southeastern Arizona). Topographic, climatic, and other maps are in the recent and available volume, *Arizona, Its People and Resources* (Cross, 1960). Fenneman (1931) is a standard general reference for physiography in the West. Historic accounts, usually illustrated, of the more recent changes in Arizona's landscapes and natural vegetation cover are given by several investigators.[6] There are numerous references (in addition to those noted above) which are primarily descriptive ecological studies on the vegetation and/or flora of Arizona.[7]

Rydberg (1913-1917) published a series of seven notable papers in the Bulletin of Torrey Botanical Club, entitled "Phytogeographical Notes on the Rocky Mountain Region." The extensive publications of the Rocky Mountain Forest and Range Experiment Station, Ft. Collins, Colorado (formerly at Tucson, Arizona), should be consulted in addition to those station papers referred to here.

Succession

The term "forest type" is generally used by foresters for a unit characterized by uniformity in composition of tree species; and "vegetation type" for any form of vegetation whether tree-form or not. "Forest type" (and "vegetation type") is equivalent to the ecological term "association" and to "consociation" where only one species is dominant. Figure 46 is of

---

[6] For example, Bryan (1928), Shreve (1929), Pearson (1931), Shreve and Hinkley (1937), Parker (1945), Brown (1950), Glendening (1952), Parker and Martin (1952), Humphrey (1953b, 1958), Schroeder (1953), Arnold and Schroeder (1955), Schulman (1956), Humphrey and Mehroff (1958), Hastings (1959), Lowe (1959a), Murray (1959), Cooper (1961), Yang (1961), Marshall (1962), and others. See Campbell and Bomberger (1934), Norris (1950), Gardner (1951), Branscomb (1958), Yang (1961), and others, for adjacent New Mexico.

[7] "Lowlands" refers here to desert and grassland habitats; "Highlands" refers to chaparral, woodland, forest, and alpine tundra. *Lowlands:* Loew (1875), Lloyd (1907), Thornber (1910), Spalding (1909, 1910), Harshberger (1911), Blumer (1912), Shreve (1915, 1925, 1942b, 1951), Aldous and Shantz (1924), Hanson (1924), Shantz and Zon (1924), Shantz and Piemeisel (1925), Sturdevant (1927), McKee (1934), Gloyd (1932, 1937), Woodbury and Russell (1945), Munz and Keck (1949), Spangle (1949), Leopold (1950), Merkle (1952), Sutton (1952), Deaver and Haskell (1955), Wallmo (1955), Yang and Lowe (1956), Yang (1957), Haskell (1958), Keppel, *et al.* (1958-60), Lowe (1959a, 1961). *Highlands:* Loew (1875), Hoffman (1877), Britton (1889), Rusby (1889), Leiberg, Rixon and Dowell (1904), Blumer (1909, 1910, 1911), Harshberger (1911), Woolsey (1911), Read (1915), Shreve (1915, 1919), Eastwood (1919), Pearson (1920, 1931, 1933, 1942, 1950), Hanson (1924), McHenry (1932, 1933, 1935), Croft (1933), Dodge (1936), Gloyd (1932, 1937), Howell (1941), Little (1941), Rasmussen (1941), Martin and Fletcher (1943), Baker (1945), Woodbury and Russell (1945), Arnberger (1947), Woodbury (1947), Peattie (1953), Dickerman (1954), Wallmo (1955), Marshall (1956), Cooper (1961a), Lowe (1961), Jameson, Williams and Wilton (1962).

Jaeger's book on The North American Deserts (Stanford University Press, 1957) is based importantly, and without due credit, on the work of Forrest Shreve.

an *association* that is a common forest type, the fir type (or Douglas fir type). Figure 48 is of a *consociation* that is a common forest type, the aspen type (or quaking aspen type).

Foresters also use the terms "temporary" and "permanent" for *successional* and *climax* stages, respectively. Thus the aspen type (Fig. 48) is a temporary forest type and the fir type (Fig. 46) is a permanent type. Aspen is temporary because it will be replaced in time by conifers, to form a permanent fir type, spruce type, or pine type, as the case may be. The succession takes place after the "permanent" climax trees have been removed, as by fire, logging, etc.; grasses ordinarily establish first, followed by the aspens and eventually by the conifers. Succession is the rule in the forest, woodland, and grassland, but not in desert. In the desert, succession is the rare exception (see Shreve, 1925; Lowe, 1959a).

The Climax Pattern

The climax is the particular pattern of the recognizably mature, characteristic vegetation and associated animals of the biotic community; that is, the natural climax pattern, or climax community pattern. The climax pattern of a geographic area is comprised of one, two, or more climax biotic associations, all of which are characterized by shared distinctiveness in *life-form* (or of strikingly different life-form) of the important climax species. Each of these biotic associations (when there is more than one) varies obviously from the other(s) in the *species composition* of its own particular climax community.

Thus there may be (1) only one climax biotic association in the area that is present on all sites, as is so often the case within areas of extensive forest (*e.g.*, in western spruce-alpine fir forest, eastern beech-maple forest); or, (2) the climax pattern may have a larger inherent genetic variation and be comprised of two or more climax biotic associations which may vary greatly in species composition (and possibly life-form) from one physical habitat site to another adjacent one within a given geographic area under the same climate; this is usually the situation in the desert (*e.g.*, Sonoran Desert, Fig. 7 and 8; see Yang and Lowe, 1956).

The climax pattern of a forest on a mountain is likely to be in the form of a *continuum* on the moisture-temperature gradient that is present; that is, a continuum of gradually changing genetic composition and life-form complexity from one extreme of the environmental gradient to the other. A climax pattern in the desert is just as likely to be one of a *mosaic* of climax species and life-forms (biotic association) as it is to be a continuum; that is, a mosaic of abruptly changing genetic composition and life-form complexity under the same climate. Hence often, as in the desert, there is abrupt repetition of climax biotic associations in the emerging form of a huge and irregular environmental chessboard on which the plants and animals are the pawns of the paired controls of topography and soil under the same climate.

This individualistic nature of the community and climax pattern was first reported very astutely and clearly by Forrest Shreve (1914, 1915) nearly a half-century ago (see also Shreve 1917, 1919, 1925, 1951). It was also ably championed by Gleason (1917, 1926, and elsewhere), Law (1929), and others in this country and abroad. But not until relatively recently has it been comprehended (or admitted) widely among American ecologists (Cain, 1939; Muller, 1939, 1940; Mason, 1947; Egler, 1951; Curtis and McIntosh, 1951; Whittaker, 1951, 1957; Brown and Curtis, 1952; Lowe, 1959a). For the somewhat older, organismic idea in American ecology, see Weaver and Clements (1938) or Allee, et al. (1949); also Kendeigh (1961).

The Climate

An understanding of the biotic communities, and the life-zones in Arizona which they comprise, is facilitated by an understanding of the physical factors which ultimately control them, particularly those of climate. A brief consideration of climate and other controlling environmental factors is presented at various places below (see Sequence of Biotic Communities and Zones). Kincer (1941), Smith (1956), Keppel, et al. (1958-60), Sellers (1960a, 1960b), and Green (1961) provide detailed climatological data and information for Arizona. The Climate of Arizona by Sellers (1960b) is a particularly informative paper on the weather elements and pertinent topographic features of the state (Fig. 1).

All of Arizona falls under the Southwestern or Arizona climatic pattern (Kincer, 1922), which is a bi-seasonal regime characterized by winter precipitation, spring drought, summer precipitation, and fall drought (Reed, 1933, 1939; Alexander, 1935; Holzman, 1937; Turnage and Mallory, 1941; Dorroh, 1946; Ives, 1949; Jurwitz, 1953; Sellers, 1960a). For most plants and animals the fore-summer drought which is associated with higher temperatures (May-June) is the more severe of the two drought periods.

The moisture for the state's bi-seasonal regime comes from northerly directions in the winter and from southerly directions in the summer. The summer precipitation comes from storms which are primarily convectional in nature, often intense, and characteristically local rather than widespread, with most storms having a diameter of less than three miles. This results from moist tropical air which moves into the state from the southeast (Gulf of Mexico, Atlantic Ocean) and the southwest (Gulf of California, Pacific Ocean) and then passes over strongly heated and mountainous terrain which causes it to rise rapidly, cool, and condense.

Summer rainfall in Arizona is from mid-May to mid-October, although the two driest months (May and June) are usually rainless. The summer monsoon begins dramatically in early July (or, less frequently, in late June), suddenly breaking the fore-summer drought and Arizona's

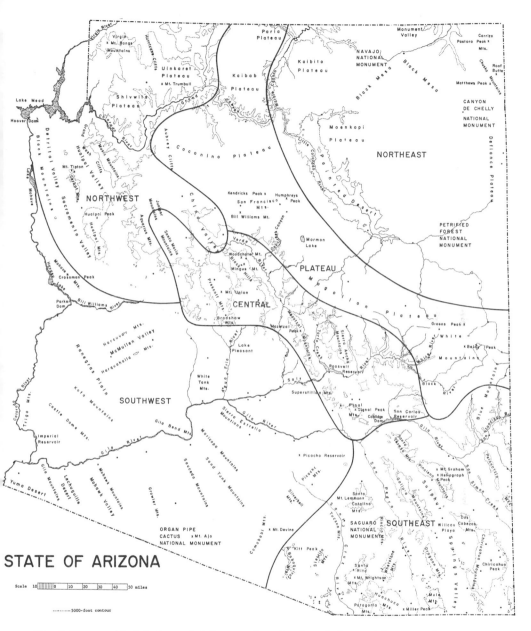

Fig. 1. Topographical features of Arizona and section boundaries used for discussion of the climate of Arizona by Sellers (1960b).

hottest weather of June-July. The major source of this precipitation throughout the summer is the Tropical Atlantic (Gulf) air mass, but in late summer (late August, September, early October) surges of moisture also may move into the state from the Tropical Pacific and contribute sizeable storms. These may be the fringes of Mexican west coast hurricanes.

The winter precipitation is associated with the westerlies which normally bring Polar Pacific air moisture onto the continent in Washington and Oregon, and occasionally do so as far south as central California. Accordingly, the convergent winter storms from the northwest (NW, N, W) may or may not pass over Arizona. When they do, surface thermal heating is obviously much less pronounced than in the case of summer conditions, upslope air movement is relatively slow, cloudiness is widespread, and the precipitation tends to be more gentle and to cover more area per storm.

In spite of the seasonal differences in storm types which are predominantly general in winter and local and erratic in summer, the winter precipitation in Arizona is decidedly more variable from year to year; it is more variable both in amount and in time of occurrence than that of the summer with its remarkably sharp onset in early July (McDonald, 1956).

In Arizona and neighboring southwestern areas, the total precipitation increases on mountain gradients at a rate of approximately 5 (4-5) inches per 1,000 feet increase in elevation (Shreve, 1915; Pearson, 1920; Sykes, 1931, Hart, 1937; Schwalen, 1942; Lull and Ellison, 1950). At the higher and usually more humid elevations, however, yearly variation is less than at the lower and ordinarily more arid levels; this relationship is also seen when comparing the eastern (more humid) and western (more arid) United States.

ECOLOGIC CHECK LIST

An ecologic check list for Arizona is given in Table 1. It is illustrated in Figures 2-53, and is annotated in the captions of the figures. Six world *ecological formation-classes*, and ten major subcontinental ecological *formations* of North America, are represented in the landscapes of Arizona.[8]

World Formation-classes

Desertscrub, grassland, chaparral, woodland, forest, and tundra landscapes are found on various continents throughout the world. These are the major types of ecological (=plant-animal, or biotic) formations, *i.e.*, the formation-classes are the principal *biotic communities* of the world. As usual in ecology, they are classified primarily on the basis of vegeta-

---

[8] For the world phytogeographic picture see Cain (1944), Good (1947), and Dansereau (1957). For the zoogeographical realms of the world (Sclater, 1858; Wallace, 1876) see Darlington (1957) and, for a brief outline, Storer and Usinger (1957).

tion (and climate) rather than animals.[9] They are occasionally called "biomes," or "biome-types."

Desertscrub

Arid, hot (or hot and cold; or cool) environments with irregular winter rainfall, summer rainfall, or bi-seasonal rainfall, which vary from (1) open, often-thorny (spinose) microphyllous *short-tree and shrub* (and other scrub) vegetation; (2) open, well-spaced microphyllous *shrub* (and other, often-thorny scrub) vegetation predominant or exclusive; to (3) *none.* Plant life-form is highly varied with leafless, drought deciduous, and evergreen species, including trees and shrubs, herbs and grasses, yuccas and agaves, cacti and ocotillo, and other, occasionally bizarre, forms.

Grassland

Semi-arid to semi-humid, warm to cold environments: (1) semi-arid *steppe, plains,* or *desert-grassland* with short grasses predominant, and occasionally scattered scrub (shrubs, yuccas, agaves, cacti, etc.); (2) semi-arid to semi-humid *savana grassland* with scattered trees and shrubs; (3) semi-humid *prairie grassland* of tall and/or mid grasses; (4) semi-humid and low temperature *mountain grassland* (mountain meadow) with short grasses and sedges.

Chaparral

Semi-arid (usually), warm to cool environments with dense, and usually closed, short-statured, mostly shrubby evergreen vegetation dominated by usually sclerophyllous, small-leaved to broad-leaved (1) shrubs, or (2) shrubs and dwarf trees (commonly scrub oaks); one species commonly dominates.

Woodland

Semi-arid to semi-humid, warm to cold environments with a more or less open canopy of (1) *evergreen* trees which are primarily species of oak, juniper, pinyon pines, and other similar life-forms, with an undergrowth of grasses and (a) woodland evergreen (often deciduous) shrubs and dry-tropic (usually deciduous) scrub, and/or (b) desert scrub (evergreen, deciduous, or leafless shrubs, cacti, yuccas, etc.); or (2) *deciduous broadleaf riparian* trees such as species of cottonwood, willow, ash, walnut, sycamore, alder, chokecherry, mulberry.

Forest

Semi-humid (occasionally semi-arid) to wet, and cold to warm environments with a more or less closed stand of trees forming a more or less continuous canopy: (1) *tropical rain forest* of tall stature, with variously shaped luxuriant foliage, in more or less continuously warm and

---

[9] In addition, I would follow Dansereau (1957) and consider the formation-classes as major subdivisions (or equivalents in part) of earth biochores; but of these three — rather than four — as follows: Forest biochore, Savana biochore, and Desert biochore.

Table 1. Check List of Biotic Communities in Arizona
and Their Major Subdivisions

Desert Formation-class
   1. *Southwestern Desertscrub* Formation*
      Creosotebush associations
       Tarbush   ,,
       Whitethorn   ,,
       Sandpaperbush ,,
       Joshuatree   ,,
       Blackorush   ,,
       Saltbush   ,,
       Paloverde   ,,
       Mesquite   ,,
   2. *Great Basin Desertscrub* Formation†
      Sagebrush associations
      Blackbrush   ,,
      Shadscale   ,,

Grassland Formation-class
   3. *Desert-Grassland* Formation‡
      Desert-Grass associations
   4. *Plains Grassland* Formation
      Shortgrass Plains associations
   5. *Mountain Grassland* Formation
      Mountain Grass associations

Chaparral Formation-class
   6. *Chaparral* Formation
      Interior Chaparral associations

Woodland Formation-class
   7. *Evergreen Woodland* Formation
      Oak Woodland associations
      Oak-pine Woodland associations
      Juniper-pinyon Woodland associations
   8. *Decidious Woodland* Formation
      Riparian Woodland associations

Forest Formation-class
   9. *Coniferous Forest* Formation
      Ponderosa Pine Forest associations
      Douglas Fir Forest   ,,
      Limber Pine Forest   ,,
      Spruce-alpine fir Forest ,,
      Aspen associes   ,,

Tundra Formation-class
   10. *Alpine Tundra* Formation
      Alpine Tundra associations

wet environments; (2) *tropical deciduous forest* of short to medium stature, with broad and small leaves that fall during the *dry* season; (3) *temperate deciduous forest* with broad leaves that fall during the *cold* season; (4) *broad-leaved evergreen forest* with variously textured broad leaves, irregular leaf-fall and generally mild cold season; (5) *needle-leaved evergreen (coniferous) forest* dominated by pines, firs, spruces, hemlocks, etc., in ordinarily semi-humid or humid, temperate to cold environments.[10]

Tundra

Cold, treeless, high latitude and high elevation environments: (1) *arctic tundra* vegetation (primarily sedges, lichens, mosses, grasses, herbs, and low shrubs) and associated animals occur characteristically over extensive plains-like landscapes with an underlying soil permafrost, and under an arid to semi-arid climate, with low precipitation, relatively high atmospheric pressure and oxygen concentration; (2) *alpine tundra* vegetation (primarily sedges, grasses, and herbaceous forms) and associated animals occur above timberline on the tops of higher mountains (at approximately 11,000-11,500 feet elevation in Arizona and New Mexico), on ordinarily shallow, mostly rocky, often unstable soils (without permafrost) under relatively humid climatic conditions with high precipitation and relatively low atmospheric pressure and oxygen concentration.

Rocky Mountain Biotic Communities

The primary characteristic biotic communities in the southern Rocky Mountains (or Southern Rocky Mountain Province) are given in Table 2. The southern Rockies are here considered as extending from their southernmost outliers, for example in southern New Mexico (Sacramento Mountains), southern Arizona (Santa Catalina-Rincons), and southern Nevada (Charleston Mountains), northward to the latitude of mid-Wyoming. All of the southernmost Rockies lie north of the Sierra Madre Occidental, and within the United States. Some of these communities (Table 2) also occur farther northward in the Rockies and some of them southward into Mexico. Table 2 for the southern Rockies may be compared with Table 1

---

[10] The classification of the world's forests is particularly complicated by their tremendous structural diversity. No brief ecologic classification, of course, is wholly representative of any formation-class.

Footnotes here refer to Table 1, page 12

*Mohave Desert, Sonoran Desert, and Chihuahuan Desert (Shreve, 1942a, 1942b, 1951). These are Scrub associations; those dominated by creosotebush, for example, may be termed the Creosotebush Scrub associations, etc.

†Great Basin Desert (Shreve, 1942b).

‡The mythical Desert-Grassland is listed as a formation merely to follow convention. It is a transitional region (ecotone) with a transitional climate between grassland and desert (Shreve, 1942a, b, c); it is, incidentally, misunderstood by many American ecologists and often misinterpreted.

for Arizona and with Daubenmire's earlier concept of the ecologic formations and "zones" involved (1943b).

A somewhat less than primary but nevertheless characteristic forest type in the Rocky Mountains is also listed for completeness, the limber pine forest· (Pearson, 1931). Limber pine and bristlecone pine form conspicuous high elevation pine communities, either as (1) associations with both species present or (2) consociations dominated by one or the other species, as discussed below under spruce-fir forest (Hudsonian Life-zone).

Table 2. The Primary Characteristic Biotic Communities in the Southern Rocky Mountains

See Table 1	Daubenmire, 1943b
Alpine Tundra	Tundra Formation
	Alpine tundra zone
Coniferous Forest	Needle-Leaved Forest Formation
Spruce-alpine fir Forest	Englemann spruce-subalpine fir zone
Limber pine Forest	Douglas fir zone
Douglas fir Forest	Ponderosa pine zone
Ponderosa pine Forest	Juniper-pinyon zone
	Oak-mountain mahogany zone
Evergreen Woodland	
Juniper-pinyon Woodland	
Oak Woodland	
Oak-pine Woodland	
Chaparral	
Interior Chaparral	
Grassland	Grassland and Desert Formations
Mountain Grassland	
Plains Grassland	
Desert-Grassland	
Desert	
Great Basin Desertscrub	
Southwestern Desertscrub	

Both pines reach their southernmost limits in Arizona; limber pine reaches its northerly limit in Alberta, bristlecone pine in Colorado. These communities are characteristic of wind-swept ridges and cold canyon heads at high elevations, and often cover entire slopes at elevations of 10,000 feet and above. Collectively they may be termed limber pine forest or limber pine-bristlecone pine forest (or, Southwestern high pine forest).

Nichol (1937) considered all of Arizona's coniferous forests as a single "Douglas fir — ponderosa pine type." While this obviously does not represent the actual vegetation of Arizona, it was adequate for a map of the vegetation of the entire United States by Schantz and Zon (1924; and Schantz, 1936), who were followed by Nichol without further detail for Arizona.

ARIZONA LIFE-ZONES

The vertically arranged zones of plant and animal life which occur in the region of the San Francisco Peaks in central Arizona were studied by C. Hart Merriam and his associates in 1889. These particular vertical zones of life, ranging between 3,000 and nearly 13,000 feet, were mapped (on the basis of vegetation) by Merriam (1890). Annotated lists of amphibians, reptiles, birds, and mammals of the region were also included. This was the beginning of the *life-zone system* which was developed by Merriam between 1890 and 1910 and continued by many others.[11] It continues to be used by biologists who live and work in Western North America.[12]

The studies noted are representative. There are many other excellent papers.[13] Probably its straightforward simplicity and verifiability are principal reasons for the vitality of the life-zone system and its continued use in the West by professional and non-professional naturalists alike (Jenks, 1931; Brandt, 1951; Heald, 1951; Arnberger, 1952; Patraw, 1953; Olin, 1959, 1961).

The number of classified zones is few (six in Arizona; Table 3) and they refer to obvious, easily observed vertical and latitudinal zones of plants and associated animals. Today, just as yesterday, these zones are based on the actually observable ecologic distribution of plants and animals and are mapped on the basis of the vegetation. They were not originally conceived (Merriam, 1890) nor followed (*e.g.*, Hall and Grinnell, 1919) and are not now recognized on the basis of temperature, moisture, or other physical factor(s), or "fauna" alone, contrary to what some would lead others to believe (see Allee, 1926; Shelford, 1932, 1945; Kendeigh, 1932, 1954, 1961).[14] The most competent, proper and

---

[11] For example, Stejneger (1893), Townsend (1893), Miller (1895, 1897), Cockerell (1897, 1898, 1900), Osgood (1900), Bailey (1902), Brown (1903), Bailey (1913, 1926; 1929,.1931, 1935, 1936), Grinnell (1908, 1928, 1935), Smith (1908), American Ornithologists' Union (1910), Cary (1911, 1917), ·Wooton and Standley (1913), Swarth (1914, 1920), Rydberg (1916), Howell (1917), Hall and Grinnell (1919), Johnson (1919), Howell (1921, 1938), Saunders (1921), Nelson (1922), Preble and McAtee (1923), Grinnell and Storer (1924), Jepson (1925), Grinnell, Dixon and Linsdale (1930), Mead (1930), van Rossem (1931, 1932, 1936a, b, 1945), McHenry (1932, 1934), Pearson (1933), Willett (1933).

[12] For example, Hargrave (1933a, b, 1936), Lutz (1934), Garth (1935, 1950), Vorhies, Jenks and Phillips (1935), Dodge (1936, 1938), Jones (1936, 1938), Gloyd (1937), Grater (1937), Graham (1937), Miller (1937, 1946, 1951), Cockerell (1941), Cooke (1941), Monson and Phillips (1941), Peterson (1941, 1942), Ball, Tinkham, Flock, and Vorhies (1942), Huey (1942), Monson (1942), Sutton and Phillips (1942), Aldrich and Friedman (1943), Hall (1946), Soper (1946), Ingles (1947), Dalquest (1948), Johnson, *et al.* (1948), Stebbins (1949, 1954), Little (1950), Murie (1951), Durrant (1952), Musebeck and Krombein (1952), Hoffmeister (1955), Cockrum (1955, 1963), Haskell (1955), Baker (1956), Castetter (1956), Van Tyne and Berger (1959), Phillips and Monson (1963).

[13] In investigations of the Olympic Peninsula and Mount Rainier, Jones (1936, 1938) determined the zonal percentages of the life-form classes in the Raunkiaeran system (see Cain, 1950).

Table 3. Temperatures (°F) in Biotic Communities in Northern Arizona in Winter (January) and in Summer (July). Data from Pearson (1920) for 1917 and 1918, and from U.S. Climatological Data (1917, 1918) for Needles, Calif.

Biotic Community	Mean Max.		Mean		Mean Min.		Minimum 1918	
	Jan.	July	Jan.	July	Jan.	July	Jan.	July
Desert								
Southern Desertscrub (Needles, 480 ft.) Lower Sonoran Life-zone	—	—	47	93	—	—	28	64
Grassland								
Desert-Grassland (Kingman, 3,300 ft.) Upper Sonoran Life-zone	54	98	41	83	28	67	21	53
Woodland								
Juniper-pinyon Woodland (Ash Fork, 5,100 ft.) Upper Sonoran Life-zone	49	90	34	74	20	59	0	50
Forest								
Ponderosa pine Forest (Flagstaff 6,900 ft.) Transition Life-zone	38	78	24	65	9	51	−13	42
Douglas fir Forest (San Francisco Mt., 9,100 ft.) Canadian Life-zone	30	68	25	58	19	49	−2	43
Spruce-fir Forest (San Francisco Mt., (10,700 ft.) Hudsonian Life-zone	26	59	21	53	16	46	−6	39
Tundra								
Alpine tundra (Timberline, 11,500 ft.) Arctic-Alpine Life-zone	22	55	16	48	10	41	−3	34

unbiased criticism of Merriam and the life-zone system has been that of Daubenmire (1938). The most useful discussion of relationships between, and uses of, zone, biome, province, etc., may be found in the work of Alden Miller (1951).

It is shown in Table 3 and Table 7 that some life-zones include more than a single biotic community; that is, a life-zone may be "generic" in being a higher level of classification including two or more biotic communities. In fact, the Upper Sonoran Zone includes too much (primarily woodlands and grasslands). It should be noted, however, that while a life-zone may be equal to a major biotic community, or contain two or more major biotic communities, a life-zone does not (in the Far West) artificially cut across natural biotic communities.

The life-zone system is not of utility on a world-wide or even continental scale, and this is only one of its shortcomings from philosophic and evolutionary points of view. It is imperfect, as are all ecologic classifications. Nevertheless, throughout subcontinental western North America it has provided a serviceable basis for faunal analysis and as the result of the soundness of the work of early naturalists, it has been found useful over a period of time equal to the age of American ecology itself, *i.e.,* since just before the turn of the century. As a tool, if not a completely satisfactory biogeographic system, it still endures; in short, it is simple, straightforward, and works throughout western North America.

Thus the authors of the Arizona vertebrate check lists, all of whom have studied over western landscapes for many years, are among those who are quick to point to the frequent usefulness of the life-zone system in the study of animals in the Southwest, and they use life-zone annotations. For western teachers in general, and especially for the elementary through high school grades, one can recommend the "life-zones" as a simple additional means to foster interest and understanding in the out-of-doors.

The following outline and discussion of the Merriam Life-zone System refers to the zones and their characteristics (*i.e.,* their biotic communities) as they occur in Arizona.

Lower Sonoran Life-zone

The Lower Sonoran Zone is equivalent to desert (Fig. 3-18). Parts of the three southern subdivisions of the North American Desert

---

[14] Merriam's subsequent and incorrect temperature facade (1894, 1899b), to explain control of the life-zones on an essentially one-factor basis, in no way vitiates the actual zonal distribution of plants and animals in nature, which observation, after all, is the basis for the concept of biotic belts or zones anywhere in the world where they occur. Actually, as was recently discussed elsewhere (Lowe, 1961), there is no need for either term (life-zone or biome) in the investigation of biotic communities and biogeography: the former is partly and the latter is wholly synonymous with *ecologic formation.* However, either term may be considered desirable for serving some purpose, as is the use of life-zone in the present check lists of vertebrates.

are represented in Arizona. These are the Mohave Desert, Sonoran Desert, and Chihuahuan Desert (the fourth subdivision is the more elevated Great Basin Desert which is treated in the Upper Sonoran Zone). The vegetation of all three may be collectively called the *Southwestern Desertscrub*, and that of the Great Basin Desert called the *Great Basin Desertscrub* (Fig. 26-29). A practically continuous belt of pine and juniper vegetation across the central part of the state effectively separates the two, the so-called "cold desert" (Great Basin Desertscrub) and "hot desert" (Southwestern Desertscrub).

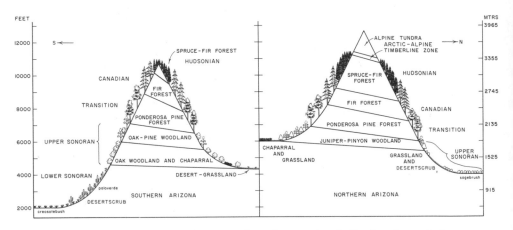

Fig. 2. Diagrammatic profiles of hypothetical mountains, indicating the vertical zonation of biotic communities in southern Arizona (left) and in northern Arizona (right). See Table 3, and text, for the corresponding life-zones.

The elevation of the zone is from 100 feet to 3,500-4,000 feet according to slope exposure; all of the life-zones extend to higher elevations on south-facing slopes than on north-facing slopes (Fig. 2). Precipitation (average annual) varies from approximately 3 to 11 inches; to about 12 inches in parts of the Chihuahuan Desert in the elevated southeastern corner of the state. It is distributed (1) primarily in winter (Mohave Desert; and Sonoran Desert, western part), or (2) more bi-seasonally (Sonoran Desert, eastern part) with somewhat more or less than half of it falling during the southwestern summer monsoon, or (3) primarily in summer (Chihuahuan Desert), with about three-quarters of the total yearly precipitation falling during the monsoon.

Desert vegetation often merges gradually, even imperceptibly, with desert-border vegetation and usually no real "line" of demarcation exists. This is particularly true, for example, in western Mexico, where there is no boundary "line" in what is a gradual south-north transition from southern subtropical thornscrub ("thorn forest") into desertscrub at the southern edge of the Sonoran Desert, in extreme southern Sonora and Baja California. This is a complex and highly informative subcontinental south-north gradient involving two primary physical controls operating on each species more or less independently of the others: these are (1) the northerly (toward U. S.) reduction in the *summer* rainfall and the total precipitation, with (2) progressively lower and critical *winter* minimum temperature. Accordingly, there is a gradual latitudinal change in community composition on this thornscrub-desertscrub environmental gradient. It involves a northward reduction in the total number of subtropical species of plants and animals as well as the amount of ground cover of the total vegetation— a progressive northward change in "openness" of the habitat, into the open and shorter-statured vegetation of the Sonoran Desert that is finally seen in southern Arizona and northwestern Sonora (Shreve, 1934).

Annual wildflowers (ephemerals) may in some years be one of the most conspicuous and colorful aspects of desert landscapes. It is well known that spring annuals (February-April) in southern Arizona may be remarkably abundant following good winter rains (from the northwest) and the plants are largely "Californian" species of mustards, poppies, sand-verbenas, etc., whereas ephemeral flower displays during July-September following good summer rains from the south are largely of "Mexican" aspect — amaranths, morning glorys, zygophylls, *et al.* Thus as one travels across the North American Desert from north to south or west to east — say, from Nevada to Sonora or from California to Chihuahua — there is an increase that one would expect in the "Mexican" component of the desert annual flower displays, just as there is in the composition of the desert perennial trees and shrubs. The plant adaptation thereby expressed is correlated with the underlying NW to SE climatic gradient away from the primarily winter (cool) precipitation of the Californian area to the predominantly summer (warm) rainfall in the Sierra Madrean area (Shreve, 1944).

It is of further interest that the more primitive relatives of many desert *annuals* are tropical and subtropical *perennial* herbs, shrubs, and trees; for example, in the families Amaranthaceae, Convolvulaceae, Hydrophyllaceae, Leguminosae, and Zygophyllaceae. This is one of numerous neontological, in addition to paleontological, relationships which are consistent with the evolutionary fact that the desert is our youngest major earth environment (see Axelrod, 1950; Shreve, 1951). And, moreover, that the ephemeral growth form (i.e., the plant life-form of holding over only as earth-covered seed) is a particularly successful one for life in harsh environments such as deserts — this is drought-evasion par excellence.

The deserts have evolved through grassland stages to the present desert conditions in response to increasing aridity since Mio-Pliocene time, and some "tougher" species of grasses still occur naturally in some of the harshest desert environments. Thus grasses may seem virtually absent over extensive areas of desert, or they may be obviously plentiful under more local conditions. Several species of *Aristida* (three-awn) are more or less successful throughout Southwestern desertscrub in Arizona.[15] The small compact desert fluff grass (*Tridens pulchellus*) in the open, and bush muhly (*Muhlenbergia porteri*) clumped around bases of shrubs, are examples of common species widely distributed but not always conspicuous throughout much of the desert. Other grasses such as big galleta (*Hilaria rigida*) and tobosa (*Hilaria mutica*) may cover conspicuously well-developed local grassland swales, which microenvironments persist well within the desert (Fig. 26). Also, on dry rocky hillsides of desert ranges which are steeply sloped, grasses occasionally may be in fair abundance as is the case with curly mesquite grass (*Hilaria belangeri*) on the Tucson Mountains and similar low ranges and desert mesas in the southern part of the state. Or, by sharp contrast, they may be next to non-existent, as are the few clumps of tanglehead grass (*Heteropogon contortus*) existing on the rugged and nearly barren volcanic desert hills in the Boulder Dam area of the Colorado River in the northwestern corner of the state.

Chihuahuan Desert

The Chihuahuan Desert is represented in Arizona by small and sometimes isolated areas in the southeastern corner of the state, primarily in Cochise County (Fig. 3-5). Parts of San Simon Valley, Sulphur Springs Valley, and San Pedro Valley have well-developed communities dominated by tarbush (*Flourensia cernua*), creosotebush (*Larrea divaricata*), sandpaperbush (*Mortonia scabrella*), or Chihuahuan white-thorn (*Acacia constrictor vernicosa*), which comprise the four major association-types of this desert occurring in Arizona. In many areas tarbush, creosotebush, and white-thorn are intermixed and associated with such species as all-thorn (*Koeberlinia spinosa*), desert sumac (*Rhus microphylla*), shrubby senna (*Cassia wislizeni*), ocotillo (*Fouquieria splendens*), mesquite (*Prosopis juliflora*), and others (Fig. 3). With the exception of creosotebush, ocotillo, and mesquite (which have wide ranges in both the Chihuahuan and Sonoran Deserts, and also occur in the Mohave Desert), these are species among a small group of plants which have wider distributions in the Chihuhuan Desert in northern Mexico and southern New Mexico, and enter only the southeastern corner of Arizona at the northwestern limits of their ranges.

The Chihuahuan Desert is essentially a shrub desert as is the Great Basin Desert. It lies mostly above 3,500 feet in elevation on the "Mexican

---

[15] In the Great Basin desertscrub scattered colonies or large populations of galleta (*Hilaria jamesi*), blue grama (*Bouteloua gracilis*), sacaton (*Sporobolus wrighti*), and three-awns (*Aristida*) are not uncommon.

Fig. 3. Southwestern Desertscrub, Chihuahuan Desert. Lower Sonoran. Looking south toward Naco Mountain, Sonora, from 4 miles NW of Naco, 4,600 ft., Cochise County. Tarbush (*Flourensia cernua*, left foreground), creosotebush (*Larrea divaricata*, right center), and white-thorn (*Acacia constricta*, small individual right foreground), with Thornber yucca (*Yucca baccata thornberi*) and grasses — a relatively mixed stand of these species, common on level valley fill.

Plateau," and the Great Basin Desert lies mostly above 4,000 feet. While it comprises small areas of Arizona, New Mexico, and Texas, it lies primarily in the states of Chihuahua and Coahuila and in parts of Durango, Zacatecas, Neuvo Leon, and San Louis Potosi. Generally lower elevations are reached in Trans-Pecos, Texas, and adjacent Chihuahua where the Chihuahuan Desert borders the Rio Grande to as low as approximately 1800 feet elevation. In several parts of Cochise County, Arizona, and in adjacent New Mexico, Western Texas, Chihuahua, and Sonora, the desert and grassland vegetations are found in complex mixtures. Desert and grassland species form interesting landscape mosaics controlled importantly by marked changes in soil conditions over very short distances.

Fig. 4. Southwestern Desertscrub, Chihuahuan Desert. Lower Sonoran. Looking northwest across San Pedro Valley, 3.5 miles E of Fairbank, Cochise County. Tar-bush, white-thorn, and creosotebush dominate the rolling, calcareous-soiled landscape in stands of various mixtures which include other shrubs and cacti: ocotillo (*Fouqueria splendens*), mariola (*Parthenium incanum*), allthorn (*Koeberlinia spinosa*), Mexican crucillo (*Condalia spathulata*), and "chollas" including Christmas cactus (*Opuntia leptocaulis*).

Grasses are more abundant in the more highly elevated Chihuahuan Desert than in the Sonoran Desert. In fact, some investigators have considered all of the Chihuahuan Desert to be a grassland climax (Weaver and Clements, 1938; Whitfield and Beutner, 1938; Whitfield and Anderson, 1938; Gardner, 1951). However it may have been in the distant past, today the Chihuahuan Desert is definitely a natural desert dominated by a host of climax shrubs (Shreve, 1917, 1939, 1942a, 1942b, 1942c; Livingston and Shreve, 1921; Shantz and Zon, 1924; Muller, 1939, 1940; Benson and Darrow, 1944; Leopold, 1950; Rzedowski, 1956). The problem is confused by the recent (historical) environmental changes and desert shrub invasions, particularly along the northern edge of the desert in the vicinity of the international boundary where the grassland and desertscrub have long met to form a mosaic landscape pattern (Shreve, 1939, 1942c; Gardner, 1951; Ditmer, 1951; Lowe, 1955; Yang, 1961).

The problem was closely examined and clearly explained by Shreve (1942c, and elsewhere). The so-called "Desert Grassland" is not merely

Fig. 5. Southwestern Desertscrub, Chihuahuan Desert. Lower Sonoran. Sandpaper-bush (*Mortonia scabrella*) in an extensive and essentially pure stand on limestone soil, Cochise County. Foreground is east edge of the town of Tombstone, 4,500 ft., looking northeastward toward Dragoon Mountains. The general appearance of this desertscrub landscape is superficially like that of chaparral.

a grassland; it is obvious also that it is not desert plains and that the term "desert plains grassland" is a poor one. This is a broad and highly varied transition region between the plains grassland (short-grass plains) and the Southwestern Desertscrub of more recent evolution (Axelrod, 1950). The climate is intermediate between desert and grassland, and a slight change in the precipitation-evaporation ratio (for example, by a slight but significant rise in evironmental temperature) can effect a pronounced change in the vegetation at a given locality.

This is happening at middle latitudes in western North America, and elsewhere, today. A small but significant climatic change toward somewhat warmer and drier conditions is "written" into diverse records (see Kincer, 1946; McDonald, 1956; Schulman, 1956).

This complex situation is to be seen on many parts of the range ecologists "beat" which lies just north of the international boundary and between southcentral Texas and southcentral Arizona, an area which has been repeatedly examined. It should be reiterated at this point that the Chihuahuan Desert lies essentially south of this transect to beyond the state of Chihuahua and into parts of Zacatecas, Durango, Nuevo Leon, and San Luis Potosi; roughly 90 per cent of it is in Mexico. Not more than a handful of ecologists have examined its southerly parts extensively or intensively; the most notable of these have been Shreve, Muller, and Rzedowski. The idea that none of the Chihuahuan Desert is desert, and that all of it is subclimax grassland (references above), is to be emphatically rejected.

Two important papers dealing with genetic variation, hybridization, and post-Pleistocene recontact of animal populations in the desert-grassland transition have been recently published (Zweifel, 1962; Dessauer, Fox, and Pough, 1962). The region investigated in southern Arizona-New Mexico is in part a complex continuum as well as mosaic transition between biotic components of the Chihuahuan Desert, Plains Grassland, and Sonoran Desert.

The Chihuahuan Desert in Arizona has a relatively poor representation of cactus life-forms and species when it is compared with the Sonoran and Mohave Deserts, but is a richer region in this regard than is the more northerly and cooler Great Basin Desert. Chollas, prickly pears, barrels, and pincushions are represented in this southeastern region of Arizona by the following more common species: cane cholla, *Opuntia spinosior;* desert Christmas cactus, *O. leptocaulis;* devil cholla, *O. stanlyi;* shrubby prickly pear, *O. macrocentra;* Engelmann prickly pear, *O. engelmanni;* Wislizenius barrel cactus, *Echinocactus wislizeni;* common pincushion, *Mammallaria vivipara aggregata;* and devil's pincushion, *Mammillaria robustispina.*

Outside of Arizona, and particularly in Mexico, there is a considerable number of other low-growing cacti, leaf succulents (*e.g.,* agaves), and stem semisucculents (yuccas) in the Chihuahuan Desert and desert-grassland. Lechugilla (*Agave lecheguilla*) and Torrey yucca (*Yucca torreyi*) are examples of these which occur as far north as southern (SW) Texas and New Mexico but which do not reach westward to Arizona.

Sonoran Desert

The Sonoran Desert covers most of southwestern Arizona. It is the hottest of our southwestern deserts, and the lowest elevation point in the State—*ca.* 100 feet on the Colorado River in "Yuma Valley"—is in this desert region. Rainfall is distinctly bi-seasonal (Arizona upland section) or occurs primarily during the winter (lower Colorado section). In Arizona the Sonoran Desert is most widely characterized by two of its principal terrestrial biotic communities, the "creosotebush communities" and the "paloverde communities."

In the paloverde-sahuaro (*Cercidium-Cereus*) community (Fig. 6, 7, 9), the plants are comprised of small-leaved desert *trees* as well as of shrubs and numerous cacti, and best development is attained on rocky hills, bajadas, and other coarse-soiled slopes in the succulent Arizona upland desert section, *e.g.,* between Ajo and Tucson. It is a particularly rich

Fig. 6. Southwestern Desertscrub. Lower Sonoran. Paloverde-sahuaro community on granite rock in Arizona Upland section of Sonoran Desert; Shreve's Ocelada Camp in Soldier Canyon, *ca.* 3000 ft., south side Santa Catalina Mountains, Pima County. In addition to foothill paloverde (*Cercidium microphyllum*) and sahuaro (*Cereus giganteus*), teddy bear cholla (*Opuntia bigelovi*), ocotillo (*Fouquieria splendens*), and brittlebush (*Encelia farinosa*) are important species in the community, particularly on south-facing slopes. Photo by Forrest Shreve, 1915. Today the Mt. Lemmon (Catalina) Highway winds upward from Soldier Trail junction, near lower right corner of picture. Few and relatively minor changes in the natural vegetation have taken place here during the past half-century.

community of desert plants and animals exhibiting highly varied and often spinose life-forms. Shrubs are more varied than the trees, and while the foothill understory may be predominantly of a single species such as triangle bur-sage (*Franseria deltoidea*) or brittlebush (*Encelia farinosa*), it is often comprised of a mixture of 5 to 15 or more shrub and dwarf shrub species in the form of a three, four or five layered understory. The primary desert (non-riparian) trees are foothill paloverde (*Cercidium microphyllum*), sahuaro (*Cereus giganteus*), ironwood (*Olneya tesota*), elephant tree (*Bursera microphylla*), crucifixion thorn (*Canotia holocantha*), desert-olive (*Forestiera phillyreoides*), holocantha (*Holocantha emoryi*),

Fig. 7. Southwestern Desertscrub, Sonoran Desert. Lower Sonoran. At 2,800 ft. near pass into Sabino Canyon, Santa Catalina Mountains. The substratum supporting the foothill paloverde community is typically rocky, being on and near the parent bedrock source of raw soil material. Life-form is highly diverse and community biomass and productivity are greater here than in the creosotebush communities on the valley fill of the plains below. This tree-dominated desert climax is not successional to, nor succeeded by, the shrub-dominated creosotebush climax desert community or any other. Photo by Forrest Shreve.

the tree-like chollas (particularly *Opuntia fulgida*), and the columnar organ-pipe cactus (*Cereus thurberi*) and senita (*Cereus schotti*).

The primarily desert *riparian* trees of the "dry" arroyos and washes include blue paloverde (*Cercidum floridum*), mesquite (*Prosopis juliflora*), catclaw (*Acacia greggi*), smoketree (*Dalea spinosa*), desert willow (*Chilopsis linearis*), jumping bean (*Sapium biloculare*), and netleaf hackberry (*Celtis reticulata*); these trees and several associated shrubs provide often well-developed riparian associations far within the desert where cottonwoods and willows (riparian woodland) do not penetrate. Such desert riparian associations are nearly as prevalent among the creosotebush as well as paloverde communities, and in the Yuma area even sahuaros, foothill paloverdes, and ironwoods are found in such arroyo habitats.

Fig. 8. Southwestern Desertscrub, Sonoran Desert. Lower Sonoran. The larger (*Larrea divaricata*) and the smaller (*Franseria dumosa*) shrubs of the creosotebush-bur-sage community on sandy soil, with no other perennial plants, as is common over extensive areas of both the Mohave and Sonoran Deserts. Yuma County, on the Yuma-San Luis Mesa, 175 ft., 7 miles E of San Luis, Arizona.

The other of the two major plant-animal communities is the much simpler creosotebush-bur sage (*Larrea-Franseria*) community (Fig. 8) which is composed mainly of *shrubs* and dwarf shrubs. Over great areas the plant dominants are essentially creosotebush (*Larrea divaricata*) and white bur-sage (*Franseria dumosa*), growing either together or alone (Fig. 10, 11). Other occasional dominants are mostly shrubs. Trees are usually lacking except for those which are desert riparian trees in the drainageways (as noted above). This shrub community characterizes habitats less rocky and of lower relief, such as valleys, mesas, and shelving plains in the lower Colorado desert section of the Sonoran Desert (the so-called "Colorado Desert"). There is often interspersion of these two major climax communities and their habitats across southwestern Arizona as may be readily observed along the highway between Yuma and Tucson, Blythe and Phoenix.

In addition to the paloverde and creosotebush associations, desert saltbush (*Atriplex polycarpa*) frequently forms extensive stands across valley bottomlands which are periodically flooded and which have soils of

Fig. 9. Southwestern Desertscrub, Sonoran Desert. Lower Sonoran. Organpipe cactus (*Cereus thurberi*) in the foothill paloverde community in Alamo Canyon, 2,400 ft., Ajo Mountains, Organ Pipe Cactus National Monument, Pima County. Triangle bur-sage (*Franseria deltoidea*) dominates the foreground.

Fig. 10. Southwestern Desertscrub, Sonoran Desert. Lower Sonoran. Pure stand of creosotebush (*Larrea divaricata*) on deep sand of the Yuma-San Luis Mesa, 150 ft., Yuma County, a few feet north of the Arizona-Sonora boundary fence, 4 miles E of San Luis del Rio Colorado, Sonora.

Fig. 11. Southwestern Desertscrub, Sonoran Desert. Lower Sonoran. Pure stand of white bur-sage (*Franseria dumosa*) on sand, one-half mile N of Dateland, 450 ft., Yuma County. This is a small stand about 300 yards diameter within the surrounding creosotebush-bur-sage community of San Cristobal Valley. Low, stabilized sand dunes on horizon are capped with western honey mesquite (*Prosopis juliflora torreyana*); dark spots in mesquites are clumps of mistletoe.

fine texture that are more or less alkaline, and saltbush (*Atriplex polycarpa*, and others) may be considered an important vegetation type in the Sonoran Desert. Mesquite (*Prosopis* spp.) formerly grew along many of the larger desert drainageways, such as those along the Gila River and some of its tributaries, in dense forest-like stands called mesquite bosques. These valuable riparian trees reached heights of 40 to 50 feet, with some individuals having trunks 2 to 3 feet in diameter. Remnants of such stands are still present in scattered areas along San Pedro River and Santa Cruz River as well as parts of the Gila and lower Colorado, and many smaller bosques still remain. In addition to the four major kinds of association-types dominated primarily by foothill paloverde, creosotebush, saltbush, and mesquite, some minor association-types in the Sonoran Desert in Arizona are dominated locally by other species such as jojoba (*Simmondsia chinensis*) on rocky upland sites within the paloverde type, white bursage (*Franseria dumosa*) within the creosotebush type, and ocotillo on elevated, rocky shallow soils; small local areas of almost pure stands of these, and some other species are occasionally encountered (Fig. 11).

Fig. 12. Southwestern Desertscrub, Sonoran Desert. Lower Sonoran. A desert wash, the usually dry bed and floodplain of the Hassayampa River at Gates Ranch, *ca.* 1750 ft., near Morristown, Maricopa County. The mesquite-acacia floodplain (mesquite bosque) is dominated by velvet mesquite (*Prosopis juliflora vetulina*). The climax of the surrounding rocky hills is paloverde-sahuaro and that of the non-riparian valley plains is creosotebush-bursage. Photo by Gerald O. Gates and E. Curtis Arnett.

Along the formerly great Gila River (the now dry bed of which stretches across the Sonoran Desert of western Arizona) there were extensive marshes, swamps, and floodplains with cattail (*Typha domingensis*), bulrush (*Scirpus olneyi*), giant reed (*Arundo donax*), common reed (*Phragmites communis*), arrowweed (*Pluchea sericea*), and many trees. The dense vegetation of these well-developed riparian communities often stood 10 to 15 feet high and supported a tremendous quantity and variety of wildlife. Today such habitats persist in modified form along the lower Colorado River and along parts of the greatly changed Gila where its remnant persists in east-central Arizona; tamarix (*Tamarix*) is an increasingly abundant foreign introduction in some of these riparian situations and may become locally undesirable.

The Sonoran Desert contains the most diverse cactus flora in our Southwest. Many species representing all of the southwestern cactus lifeforms are present: columnar and giant cactus (*Cereus*), barrels (*Echino-*

Fig. 13. Southwestern Desertscrub, Sonoran Desert. Lower Sonoran. Creosotebush on rough desert pavement, 8 miles W of Sentinel, Yuma County. Plant in foreground is partly dead and 45 per cent of the stand is completely dead today on this black, rocky surface under 3-4 inches annual rainfall. No plant succession takes place here; the same species and often the same individuals are both the pioneer and the climax plants.

cactus), chollas (*Opuntia*), prickly pears (*Opuntia*), hedgehogs and rainbows (*Echinocereus*), and the pincushions and fish hooks (*Mammillaria*). In order of decreasing richness of cacti in the flora, our deserts are: Sonoran, Mohave, Chihuahuan, Great Basin.

Mohave Desert

The Mohave Desert is a transitional area between the more highly elevated and cooler Great Basin Desert in the north and the hotter Sonoran Desert in the south. In Arizona this desert is in the western and northwestern part of the state, northward of the approximate line Needles — Congress Junction, and into the extreme northwestern corner within and north of the valley of the Grand Wash Cliffs, to (and across) the Utah state line. It covers considerably greater desert area in southeastern California, and also occurs in southern Nevada and in extreme southwestern Utah, in the Virgin River drainage to a few miles north of St. George and east of Hurricane. Most of the dominant plant species have their main distribution in the other deserts and creosotebush is the primary

Fig. 14. Southwestern Desertscrub, southern edge of Mohave Desert-Sonoran Desert transition, 12 miles NW of Congress Junction, *ca.* 3,000 ft., Yavapai County, looking eastward toward Date Creek Mountains. Lower Sonoran. Joshuatree (*Yucca brevifolia*) is a Mohave species. Foothill paloverde (*Cercidium microphyllum*), tree on left, is a Sonoran one. Creosotebush, left-center edge and across center background, is the most abundant and conspicuous plant species common to both deserts.

shrub. Open stands of creosotebush and white bur-sage occur more or less throughout. Only three plants usually stand above the generally low shrubs: Joshuatree and Mohave yucca at the somewhat higher elevations, and catclaw along washes.

The principal association-types in the Mohave Desert in Arizona are creosotebush, Joshuatree, blackbush, and saltbush; also bladder-sage. Bladder-sage (*Salazaria mexicana*) is a widespread and nearly endemic species of the Mohave Desert and in some areas it may form nearly pure stands. Other and more minor associations on the Mohave are often in transitional areas between major associations. These may be partly to almost wholly dominated by white bur-sage, shrubby buckwheat (*Eriogonum wrighti*), other shrubs (such as snakeweed) and some grasses such as big galleta (*Hilaria rigida*) and tobosa (*H. mutica*).

One of the best-known life-forms is the Joshuatree (*Yucca brevifolia*) which forms often extensive "forests" or "woodlands" of varied associations. The understory vegetation may be dominated by a shrub species of the northern desertscrub (*e.g.*, blackbrush, Fig. 17), or by one of the southern desertscrub (*e.g.*, creosotebush), or by a species more or less endemic to

Fig. 15. Southwestern Desertscrub, Mohave Desert. Lower Sonoran. Creosotebush-bur-sage with Mohave yucca (*Yucca schidigera*) and other shrubs in Detrital Valley, Mohave County. Looking westward toward Black Mountains, 21 miles NW of Chloride, *ca.* 2,400 ft.

the Mohave desert area (*e.g.*, Parish devil cholla, Fig. 18). More often, however, the plants associated with the Joshuatree are several species in various complex mixtures, with mostly Great Basin species in the northern part of the Mohave Desert and Sonoran Desert species in the southern part.

At the southern limit of the Joshuatree's distribution in Arizona, a few miles northwest of Congress Junction, Yavapai County (Fig. 14), it grows adjacent to and often in association with species of the Sonoran Desert such as foothill paloverde, sahuaro, ocotillo, and crucifixion thorn, as well as creosotebush and white bur-sage. Here, in a transitional area of Mohave desert and Sonoran desert, there are no typically Great Basin desert species (*e.g.*, sagebrush, shadscale) associated with Joshuatree.

The Mohave yucca (*Yucca schidigera*, Fig. 15) is also conspicuous over large areas of the Mohave desert where it is commonly in association with creosotebush, white bur-sage, bladder-sage (*Salazaria mexicana*), brittlebush (*Encelia farinosa*), chollas, barrels, etc. The ecologic distribution of Mohave yucca overlaps that of the Joshuatree, and while both species frequently are together, as on the upper parts of outwash slopes along the bases of desert ranges, the Mohave yucca also occurs at some-

Fig. 16. Southwestern Desertscrub, Mohave Desert. Lower Sonoran. Small trees of catclaw (*Acacia greggi*) in Detrital Wash, Detrital Valley, *ca.* 2,400 ft., Mohave County. Catclaw is one of the few desert riparian trees in the Mohave Desert, and the only one commonly seen throughout the Mohave in Arizona. It grows as a shrub in non-riparian desert habitats.

what lower elevations. Banana yucca (*Yucca baccata*) also occurs with both Mohave yucca and Joshuatree, and the three yuccas occur together at many localities in Mohave County.

Often in association with one or more of these yuccas, several life-forms of cacti are conspicuous, although cacti on the Mohave desert are by no means as varied or as numerous as in the Sonoran Desert and are largely restricted to the coarse soils on the gentle outwash slopes. These include chollas (*e.g.*, buckhorn cholla, *Opuntia acanthocarpa*; Mohave cholla, *O. echinocarpa*; shrubby cholla, *O. ramosissima*; Parish devil cholla, *O. stanlyi parishi*), prickly pears (*e.g.*, Mohave prickly pear, *Opuntia erinacea*; beaver tail cactus, *O. basilaris*; variable prickly pear, *O. phaeacantha*), hedgehog cactus (*Echinocereus engelmanni*), barrel cactus (*Echinocactus acanthodes*), and the desert pincushion (*Mammillaria vivipara deserti*). Also the sahuaro (*Cereus giganteus*) reaches its

Fig. 17. Southwestern Desertscrub, Mohave Desert, Lower Sonoran. Joshuatree "forest" (*Yucca brevifolia*) with a dense stand of blackbrush (*Coleogyne ramosissima*) interspersed primarily with banana yucca (*Yucca baccata*), *ca.* 3,400 ft., on Pierce Ferry road looking eastward toward Grand Wash Cliffs, Mohave County.

northernmost limit in the southern part of the Mohave desert, west of the Hualapai Mountains in southern Mohave County.

One of the striking differences between the Mohave desert (also Great Basin desert) and the Sonoran desert is the relative paucity of desert trees in the Mohave. Even along large arroyos and other drainageways in Mohave they are in near absence, both in kinds and in numbers of individuals. Three southerly riparian species of trees are present, however spotty in distribution, in the Mohave in Arizona: desert willow (*Chilopsis linearis*), western honey mesquite (*Prosopis juliflora torreyana*), and catclaw (*Acacia greggi*). Catclaw, either as a small tree or shrub, is the species more commonly seen throughout most of the Mohave (Fig. 16), particularly in Arizona.

Fig. 18. Southwestern Desertscrub, Mohave Desert. Lower Sonoran. Open Joshua-tree "woodland" on the Pierce Ferry Road, *ca.* 2,500 ft., Mohave County, with a conspicuous dwarf cactus "ground cover" of Parish devil cholla (*Opuntia stanlyi parishi*) interspersed with occasional creosotebush and banana yucca.

Upper Sonoran Life-zone

The Upper Sonoran Zone includes *woodland* (Fig. 33-39), *chaparral* (Fig. 32), *grassland* (Fig. 23-29) and *Great Basin desertscrub* (Fig. 19-22). Two exceptions to this "inclusion" should be noted, as follows: (1) riparian woodland (Fig. 40, 64-66), which occurs throughout all of the life-zones except the highest two, Hudsonian and Arctic-Alpine, and (2) mountain grassland (Fig. 31) which occurs in (forest) zones above the Upper Sonoran. Elevation of the zone is 3,500 to 4,000 feet to as high as 7,000 feet on some slopes. Precipitation varies from as little as 7 or 8 inches in the shrub-dominated Great Basin Desert to as much as 21 or 22 inches in tree-dominated woodland communities.

Great Basin Desert

The southeastern limit of the Great Basin desertscrub lies in the northern part of Arizona, principally in the region north and east of Flagstaff. It also occurs in areas in the extreme northwest, near the Utah State line, being particularly well represented in the Strip Country north of the Grand Canyon. This is the most highly elevated of the four deserts

Fig. 19. Great Basin Desertscrub, Great Basin Desert. Upper Sonoran. Basin sage-brush (*Artemisia tridentata*) in the Arizona Strip country north of the Colorado River. The pure stand of sagebrush is bordered on the distant horizon by juniper-pinyon woodland. Photo by Robert R. Humphrey.

(approximately 3,000 to 6,500 feet) with most of it occurring above 4,000 feet. Accordingly, it is also the coolest and it is sometimes called the cool desert, cold desert, semi-desert, etc. Precipitation is more evenly distributed throughout the year than it is in the other desert regions of the state, and is approximately 7 to 12 inches annually.

The Great Basin is a shrub (and grass) dominated desert in which the vegetation is of relatively low stature (Fig. 19-22) and is more or less uniform, with just a few species (and often only one) comprising the stand over extensive areas of similarly uniform relief. Trees are almost totally absent, and the shrubs have small leaves which are wholly or partly deciduous. The landscapes are more often spoken of as monotonous; they are, nevertheless, interesting to those who inspect them closely.

Major shrubs are big sagebrush (*Artemisia tridentata*), blackbrush (*Coleogyne ramosissima*), shadscale (*Atriplex confertifolia*), mormon-tea (*Ephedra viridis* and others), and greasewood (*Sarcobatus vermiculatus*). Each of these shrubs often forms more or less pure stands, and commonly with little more than a few associated grasses present; sagebrush, black-brush, and shadscale form the principal groups of associations in Arizona.

37

Fig. 20. Great Basin Desertscrub, Great Basin Desert. Upper Sonoran. A pure stand of shadscale (*Atriplex confertifolia*) near Fredonia, Coconino County, 5,000 ft. One of the principal shrubs of the southern part of the Great Basin Desert, shadscale covers extensive areas in essentially pure stands, as does sagebrush (*Artemisia*) and blackbrush (*Coleogyne*).

In some areas other shrubs are of occasional prominence, such as four-wing saltbush (*Atriplex canescens*), black sagebrush (*Artemisia nova*), sand sagebrush (*Artemisia filifolia*), rabbitbrush (*Chrysothamnus nauseosus*), snakeweed (*Gutierrezia sarothrae*), plateau yucca (*Yucca angustissima*), pale lycium (*Lycium pallidum*), desert olive (*Forestiera neomexicana*), and serviceberry (*Amelanchier utahensis*). Relatively few species of cacti occur in this desert in Arizona, and none appear restricted to it. The most abundant are prickly pears (*e.g.*, grizzly bear cactus, *Opuntia erinacea ursina*; Navajo prickly pear, *O. erinacea hystricina*; western prickly pear, *O. polyacantha*; fragile prickly pear, *O. fragilis*) and chollas (*e.g.*, Whipple cholla, *Opuntia whipplei*).

The region in northeastern Arizona between the Little Colorado River and the Hopi Mesas was originally named the "Painted Desert" by Geologist Newberry during Ives' (1861: 76-78) exploration of the Colorado River (Dellenbaugh, 1932; McKee, 1933).[16] The Painted Desert is a minor subdivision of the Great Basin Desert which lies along the Little Colorado River below approximately 5,000 feet (1,500 meters) in elevation as properly indicated by Merriam (1890) and by Sellers (1960). It lies in

[16] Dr. J. S. Newberry (1861) wrote the report on the geology of the Ives Expedition to the Colorado River of the West, which constitutes Part III of the Ives Report.

Fig. 21. Great Basin Desertscrub, Great Basin Desert. Upper Sonoran. On the Arizona-Utah border, looking northwest from Comb Ridge across Monument Valley, 5,200 ft., to Navajo Mountain (the dome in the distant horizon, right center). In the immediate foreground is an open juniper-pinyon woodland along the upper edge of the desert valley. Photo by E. Tad Nichols.

eastern Coconino County, roughly between Tuba City near the northern end and Leupp near the southern end. Thus the parts of the "Painted Desert" of recent popular writers that are actually desert (*e.g.*, Jaeger, see footnote 7) lie wholly within the Great Basin Desert. Among the few species of widely scattered plants which occur at variously spaced intervals on the mostly bare ground, the most common are saltbushes (shadscale and fourwing) and grasses (primarily the dropseed grass called sacaton). The bareness of the ground (*e.g.*, north of Cameron, Coconino county) contributes to the spectacular displays of color which give this area its name of "painted," for there is widespread and almost complete exposure of the brilliantly colored soil layers of the actively eroding hills of shale (siltsone, *et al.*) which were originally laid down as old lake deposits during Upper Triassic time many millions of years ago (Fig. 22).

Fig. 22. Great Basin Desertscrub, Great Basin Desert. Upper Sonoran. The characteristic Chinle marl of the "Painted Desert," at *ca.* 10 miles north of Cameron, 4,200 ft., Coconino County. The delicate, striking coloring of these barren eroding hills of shale led Geologist J. S. Newberry of the Ives expedition to give the name "painted desert" to this area between Leupp (northwest of Winslow) and Tuba City. This relatively small area within the Great Basin Desert lies essentially below 5,000 feet elevation in the immediate drainage of the Little Colorado River. Photo by E. Tad Nichols.

Grassland

Desert-Grassland. Desert-grassland (Fig. 23-29) is a transitional type of grass-dominated landscape commonly positioned between desert below and evergreen woodland or chaparral above. Its lower limit is about 3,500 feet elevation and its best development is between 4,000 and 5,000 feet. Most of the desert-grassland in Arizona receives 10 to 15 inches of precipitation annually; the extremes are about 9 and 18 inches with the mean lying somewhere between 12 and 15. In Arizona, it is largely contained in the southeastern quarter of the state, but also occurs in the northwestern quarter, as in the vicinity of Kingman in Mohave County (Fig. 25). The grasses are often bunch-growth perennials in which the bases of the clumps are separated by intervening bare ground.

Fig. 23. Desert-grassland. Upper Sonoran. A landscape of palmilla (*Yucca elata*) and grama grasses (*Bouteloua*) in Cochise County. This is the principal landscape (yucca-grass) which many Arizonans think of when the name "desert grassland" is used. However, the stand of grama shown here is more dense than is usual over most of the desert-grassland transition in southern Arizona today. Photo by Robert R. Humphrey.

Where soil may be deep, well-protected from erosion and with few rocks, shrubs, or cacti, perennial grama grasses such as black grama (*Bouteloua eriopoda*), blue grama (*B. gracilis*), sideoats grama (*B. curtipendula*), slender grama (*B. filiformis*), and hairy grama (*B. hirsuta*) may cover, even today, extensive stretches of landscape. Many other grasses are mixed with the gramas, e.g., plains lovegrass (*Eragrostis intermedia*), plains bristlegrass (*Setaria machrostachya*), sand dropseed (*Sporobolus cryptandrus*), and cottongrass (*Trichachne californica*), and several species of three-awn (*Aristida*).

Such purely grass landscapes, however, stand in marked contrast to other desert-grassland cover on much of the shallow-soiled, rocky and gravelly hills and slopes which are of considerable extent in these parts of Arizona. On such shallower soils the climax grasses are usually much reduced and some of them eliminated in competition with a wide variety of shrub, tree, and cactus life-forms such as prickly pears and chollas, agaves, yuccas, ocotillo, fairy duster, wait-a-minute bush, cat-claw, and mesquite. Sotol (*Dasylirion wheeleri*) and beargrass (*Nolina microcarpa*) are shrub life-forms which are occasionally conspicuous and may even

41

Fig. 24. Desert-grassland. Upper Sonoran. Thornber yucca (*Yucca bacata thornberi*) in a nearly pure stand extends as far as the eye can see. A few widely scattered palmilla and sotol (*Dasylirion wheeleri*) also occur and the small-clumped fluff grass (*Tridens pulchellus*) is a predominant species. Looking southwestward toward Mount Fagan from near Mountain View (between Tucson and Benson), *ca.* 3,600 ft., Pima County.

dominate local situations on shallow soils. Only the tougher grasses (that are, incidentally, of lesser forage value) may be present or abundant, such as ring grass (*Muhlenbergia torreyi*), red three-awn (*Aristida longiseta*), and fluff-grass (*Tridens pulchellus*). Mesquite has invaded large areas of former grassland as have other trees (*e.g.*, juniper) and some shrubs both native and introduced. Investigations have included before-and-after photographs which are especially informative aids, *e.g.*, the photographs of Parker and Martin (1946) for grass stand in 1903 to mesquite stand in 1941 on the north side of the Santa Rita Mountains.

The extremes of the desert-grassland in Arizona have just been briefly noted, *i.e.*, (1) grass landscapes of essentially pure stands of grasses and (2) the other more frequent extreme of mixed grass-shrub landscapes, often expressed as shrub and/or tree stands with varying grass composition and depletion. Between these extremes, two very characteristic desert-grassland habitats in Arizona today are represented by (1) extensive yucca-grass landscapes on undulating terrain (Fig. 23, 24) and (2) tobosa

Fig. 25. Desert-grassland. Upper Sonoran. Looking northwestward, 3,400 ft., across Hualapai Valley toward Cerbat Mountains which extend northward from Kingman, Mohave County. The shrubs, yuccas, and cacti as well as the grasses in this desert-grassland in Mohave and Yavapai counties are often of the same genera and species as those of the similar desert-grassland in southeastern Arizona.

grass (*Hilaria mutica*) in flat valley bottomlands and swales (Fig. 26). The differences in plant life-form as well as plant and animal species which occur in these two characteristic kinds of southwestern biotic communities are the result of the differences in topography, run-off, and soil character-istics which prevail in an extensive habitat mosaic under the same macro-climate.

Plains Grassland. Well developed plains grassland, in which the grasses form a continuous or nearly uninterrupted cover, occurs in Arizona generally between 5,000 and 7,000 feet elevation and essentially in the eastern half of the state. Most of it receives 11 to 18 inches of annual precipitation, with extremes of approximately 10 and 21 inches.

San Rafael Valley in Santa Cruz County (Fig. 30), parts of Sulfur Springs Valley in Cochise County, and isolated Chino Valley in Yavapai County are examples of plains grassland habitats carpeted with species of grama grass (*Bouteloua*), muhly (*Muhlenbergia*), needlegrass (*Stipa*), dropseed (*Sporobolus*), sprangletop (*Leptochloa*), and others.

43

Fig. 26. Desert-grassland isolated in the Sonoran Desert. Lower Sonoran. Tobosa grass (*Hilaria mutica*), foot-high, in the swale of a periodically flooded desert valley at Ventana Ranch, 2,100 ft., roughly midway between Ajo and Sells, in *southwestern* Arizona. A few large palmilla (*Yucca elata*) remain in parts of this tobosa swale which is surrounded by desertscrub of creosotebush, paloverde, sahuaro, *et al.* on higher (coarser-soiled and better-drained) ground. This tobosa landscape, on bottom-land, is a principal one in the desert-grassland (Upper Sonoran) in *southeastern* Arizona; e.g., in Cochise County, where such swales are surrounded by other desert-grassland habitats (as in Figures 23 and 24). The dark vegetation line across the "skyline" is a distant mesquite bosque.

In northeastern Arizona, particularly in Navajo and Apache Counties, the formerly extensive plains grassland is now much reduced. There the native grasses are mostly species of grama (*Bouteloua*), fescue (*Festuca*), dropseed (*Sporobolus*), wheatgrass (*Agropyron*), muhly (*Muhlenbergia*), and brome (*Bromus*); galleta (*Hilaria jamesi*) is also one of the characteristic species and its counterpart in the southeastern desert-grassland is tobosa (*Hilaria mutica*). Plains grassland is a semi-arid grassland habitat which occasionally extends upward into the lower portion of the Transition Zone (ponderosa pine forest) in northern Arizona, and is also often in various mixtures with juniper-pinyon woodland and sagebrush.

Fig. 27. Desert-grassland, Upper Sonoran, Empire Mountains, 12 miles southeast of Vail, Pima County, *ca.* 4100 ft., looking southeast across Davidson Canyon toward highest Empire Peak, March 21, 1915. In immediate foreground is a "Rogues gallery of noxious invaders" of the grassland: from left to right, Thornber yucca (*Yucca baccata thornberi*), cane cholla (*Opuntia spinosior*), velvet mesquite (*Prosopis juliflora vetulina*), prickly pear (*Opuntia engelmanni*), Parry agave (*Agave parryi*), ocotillo (*Fouqueria splendens*), and white-thorn (*Acacia constricta*). In background are larger mesquites (deciduous), Mexican crucillos (*Condalia spathulata*, evergreen), and one-seed juniper (*Juniperus monosperma*, evergreen).   Today at this locality, which can be viewed from State Highway 83 between Vail and Sonoita, there is an obvious increase of the dry-tropic·scrub invaders on the bajada, in the draws and on the lower slopes, unquestionably at the expense of the perennial grasses of forage value. Photo by Forrest Shreve.

Fig. 28. Desert-grassland. Upper Sonoran. A desert-like landscape on a rocky south-facing slope within the desert-grassland, 17 miles N of Sonoita, *ca.* 4,000 ft., in Pima County. Grasses are virtually lacking and ocotillo and prickly-pear are conspicuous, as is commonly the case on such sites today. Other shrubs and cacti here are golden-flowered agave, sotol, mesquite, Mexican crucillo, white-thorn, chollas and barrel cactus.

Fig. 29. Desert-grassland. Upper Sonoran. Sand sage (*Artemisia filifolia*) within the desert-grassland on deep, fine sand along the eastern edge of Willcox Playa, *ca.* 4,200 ft., Cochise County; looking eastward toward the Dos Cabezas Mountains. A few large mesquites and a tall palmilla are conspicuous.

Fig. 30. Plains Grassland. Upper Sonoran. San Rafael Valley, 5,000 ft., east of Lochiel, Santa Cruz County. Looking southwestward into Sonora from south side of Huachuca Mountains near mouth of Parker Canyon.

Mountain Grassland. Mountain grassland occurs in relatively small areas which are natural openings in coniferous forest. These are found from the ponderosa pine forest well into spruce-alpine fir forest. Greatest development is reached in the White Mountains, *e.g.*, the "prairies" of the Apache National Forest, and on the Kaibab Plateau (Fig. 31). It is also fairly well represented in some of the higher isolated mountain ranges in southern Arizona such as the Pinaleno Mountains and Chiricahua Mountains. The forest edge is well marked where the two habitats come together and produce the forest "edge effect." The soils have relatively high rates of moisture evaporation, and obviously have physical properties unsuitable for tree growth.

The characteristic grasses include mountain timothy, Arizona fescue, mountain muhly, pine dropseed, black dropseed, needlegrass, mountain brome, Arizona wheatgrass, and the introduced Kentucky bluegrass. Herbs are common and during the summer beautiful fields of flowers may rise above the green grass carpet. This is particularly true in the Transition and Canadian Life-zones. At higher elevations, where these "mountain meadows" border spruce-fir forest, the wetter (lower) sites are often actually dominated by a considerable number of mostly low-growing herbs instead of by the grasses and sedges; the somewhat drier (higher) drainage sites are those dominated by the grasses and grass-like species.

Chaparral

Interior chaparral occurs in Arizona[17] in the central part of the state, usually between 4,000 and 6,000 feet elevation, from the foothills below the Mogollon Rim to somewhat south of the Gila River, and from the eastern border of the state westward, in progressively smaller areas, into Mohave County where it is fairly well developed as far west as the Hualapai Mountains. Small stands may occur to as low as 3,500 feet and to as high as 7,000 feet, and precipitation ranges from approximately 13 to 23 inches annually. The physiognomy of chaparral is that of dense shrubby growth, usually closed or not widely open, of fairly uniform height between 3 and 6 or 7 feet, broken by an occasional taller shrub or short tree. In Arizona, fairly uniform tall stands of curl-leaf mountain mahogany (*Cercocarpus ledifolius*) may reach over 10 feet in height.

The dominant plants are generally tough-leaved evergreen shrubs. Scrub oak (*Quercus turbinella*) is by far the most common dominant and it may account for over 90 per cent of the stand in many areas (Fig. 32); it is more than likely that it is conspecific with the common scrub oak (*Q. dumosa*) in the California coastal chaparral.

The following twenty-odd species are mostly evergreen and, with scrub oak, are among the most conspicuous or common shrubs in the Arizona chaparral: manzanita (*Arctostaphylos pungens; A. pringlei*),

---

[17] There is considerable confusion as to what constitutes chaparral in Arizona.

Fig. 31. Mountain Grassland. Hudsonian Life-zone. Looking southward in V T Park, Kaibab Plateau, north of Grand Canyon, 9,000 ft. The bordering coniferous forest is dominated primarily by blue spruce (*Picea pungens*).

Fig. 32. Chaparral. Upper Sonoran. Essentially pure stand of scrub oak (*Quercus turbinella*) on lower slopes of the Prescott Mountains, midway between Iron Springs and Skull Valley, *ca.* 5,000 ft., Yavapai County. There is slight variation in stature in this chaparral which stands between knee-height and hip-height.

sugar sumac (*Rhus ovata*), scarlet sumac (*Rhus glabra*), squawbush (*Rhus trilobata*), mountain-mahogany (*Cercocarpus breviflorus* and *C. betuloides*), buckbrush (*Ceanothus greggi*), deerbrush (*Ceanothus integerrimus*), buckthorn (*Rhamnus crocea, R. californica, R. betulaefolia*), silk-tassel (*Garrya wrighti, G. flavescens*), Apache plume (*Fallugia paradoxa*), brickellbush (*Brickellia californica*), red mahonia (*Berberis haematocarpa*), wait-a-minute bush (*Mimosa biuncifera*), mountain-balm (*Eriodictyon angustifolium*), cliffrose (*Cowania mexicana*), poison-oak (*Rhus diversiloba*) and turpentine bush (*Aplopappus laricifolius*). California fremontia (*Fremontodendron californicum*) and mock-locust (*Amorpha californica*) are shrubs of the chaparral in California and Baja California which occur also in the interior chaparral of Arizona as local species usually occurring in canyons. Sugar sumac, buckthorn, mountain-mahogany (*C. betuloides*), and brickellbush, as listed above, are among the several other disjunctive species between California coastal chaparral and Arizona interior chaparral today separated by desert.

There is no species of grass peculiar to the chaparral formation in Arizona. Grasses may be scarce in closed chaparral, yet may be abundant in open chaparral and especially so following burns. Blue, black, and sideoats grama, plains lovegrass, wolftail, cane beardgrass, red-brome, desert fluff grass, bush muhly and red three-awn are among the commonest species found either in parts of, or throughout, the chaparral.

Chaparral occurs widely in coastal California and adjacent Baja California (coastal chaparral), and under a similar effective climate in the Mediterranean region where it is called *macchie* and *garique*. Our term chaparral evolved from the Basque word *chabarra* and the later Spanish word *chaparro*, both for dwarf evergreen oaks. In the New World, the place name suffix *-al*, meaning "place of," was added and our present word chaparral resulted. It is a useful designation for a distinctive climax vegetation and biotic community occurring under a more or less distinctive climate (Cronemiller, 1942).

Evergreen Woodland

Southern Arizona. In southern Arizona the woodland trees are either mostly or wholly evergreen oaks (*Quercus*, Fig. 33). It may often be an *oak woodland* comprised primarily of Emory oak (*Quercus emoryi*, the most common species, Fig. 34). In addition, there may be Arizona oak (*Q. arizonica*), and Mexican blue oak (*Q. oblongifolia*), with alligator juniper (*Juniperus deppeana*) occasional to abundant, and one-seed juniper (*J. monosperma*) and Mexican pinyon (*Pinus cembroides*) of sporadic occurrence (encinal, Fig. 35). It is usually an open (and often very open) woodland, with numerous associated species of grasses, drytropic shrubs, succulents, and some cacti more or less prevalent throughout.

Fig. 33. Oak Woodland. Upper Sonoran. Large evergreen oaks in foreground, "Stone Cabin Canyon" (Florida Canyon) on north side Santa Rita Mountains, at *ca.* 4100 ft. In upper half of view is typical gradual transition (continuum) from (1) desert-grassland at extreme right center, through (2) open oak-grass savanna (open encinal) in center, to (3) oak woodland (dense encinal) above, on the center peaks and on slopes at extreme left center, with (4) coniferous forest on high slopes and ridges at top left. Photo by Forrest Shreve, 1911. Investigation of this area at present reveals three essential points with regard to change in the general vegetation: (1) dry-tropic shrub and tree density has increased in the desert-grassland area, with reduction of perennial grasses; (2) evergreen oaks (Emory oak, Mexican blue oak) have recently died in the marginal area of oak-grass savanna; and (3) mortality of evergreen oaks within the oak woodland community remains unchanged; there is very little deterioration within, and no decimation of, the oak woodland itself.

Fig. 34. Oak Woodland. Upper Sonoran. An extensive stand of evergreen oaks which is nearly a pure stand of Emory oak (*Quercus emoryi*), *ca.* 5,500 ft. and below, from south side Huachuca Mountains (between Moctezuma Pass and Sunnyside) southward into Sonora. Arizona oak (*Q. arizonica*) and Mexican blue oak (*Q. oblongifolia*) are also present.

Mexican oak-pine woodland lies between the oak woodland (or encinal)[18] below and the ponderosa pine forest (Transition Life-zone) above (Fig. 36). It is characterized in part both floristically and vegetatively by the presence of two large mid-elevation conifers, Chihuahua pine (*Pinus leiophylla*) and Apache pine (*Pinus engelmanni*); these species, with Mexican pinyon and alligator juniper, are variously intermingled with several species of evergreen oaks — principally silverleaf oak (*Q. hypoleucoides*), Arizona oak (*Q. arizonica*), and Emory oak (*Q. emoryi*).

All of these evergreen woodland types (oak, encinal, pine-oak) are largely dominated by species of evergreen oaks and are primarily situated in the southeastern quarter of the state south of the Gila River, where they occur on hills and mountain slopes between 4,000 and 6,500 feet (occasionally slightly higher) and reach their greatest development

---

[18] The term *encinal* refers to a primary Sierra Madrean type of woodland in the sub-Mogollon Southwest. It is dominated by oaks, junipers, and pinyons in more or less equal or subequal abundance, in which the former two or the latter two trees may predominate locally in association with a number of chaparral shrubs (Shreve, 1915; Marshall, 1957; Lowe, 1961). These papers and those of Gentry (1942) and Leopold (1950) refer also to oak-pine woodland. See in particular the excellent work of Marshall (1957).

Fig. 35. Encinal. Upper Sonoran. A rocky habitat with shallow granitic soil, south side Santa Catalina Mountains, 5,800 ft. This is a mixed evergreen woodland dominated by pinyon, oaks, and juniper. The principal tree in foreground is Mexican pinyon (*Pinus cembroides*), often more prevalent than juniper at 5,500-6,000 ft. and above. The oaks are Emory oak and Arizona oak and the juniper is alligator juniper (*Juniperus deppeana pachyphlaea*).   Shreve's term "encinal" is appropriate; it refers to Sierra Madrean evergreen woodlands that are partly or wholly dominated by evergreen oaks. This woodland has also been called "oak-juniper type"; one-seed juniper (*J. monosperma*) is the second species locally associated with evergreen oaks between 4,500 and 5,500 ft., as in the Santa Rita Mountains.

on the foothills of the larger mountains such as the Pinals, Pinalenos, Galiuros, Santa Catalinas, Baboquivaris, Santa Ritas, Huachucas, and Chiricahuas.

The shrubs which center their distributions in these oak type woodlands usually range upward into the pine forest or downward into desert grassland or both. Characteristic species are velvet-pod mimosa (*Mimosa dysocarpa*), woodland sumac (*Rhus choriophylla*), algerita (*Berberis haematocarpa*), mountain yucca (*Yucca schotti*), golden-flowered agave (*Agave palmeri*), and Parry agave (*Agave parryi*). Buckbrush (*Ceanothus fendleri*) and locust (*Robinia neomexicana*) are species occurring in the ponderosa pine forest which reach their lower elevational limits in woodland. A number of primarily chaparral shrubs may occur in parts of the oak type woodlands; buckthorn (*Rhamnus*), manzanita (*Arctostaphylos*), mountain mahogany (*Cerocarpus*), squawbush (*Rhus*), poisonoak (*Rhus*), and silktassel (*Garrya*) are representative. Some of these grow primarily under the direct canopy of the oak tree (*e.g.*, squawbush, *Rhus trilobata*), as does the native canyon grape (*Vitis arizonica*), while others grow primarily in open areas between the trees (*e.g.*, Mexican manzanita, *Arctostaphylos pungens*).

Other dry-tropic shrubs and succulents occurring to varying degrees in these interior Southwest woodlands, and which are features of the woodland at its desert or grassland edge (as is the tree *Vauquelinia californica*, rosewood), include coral-bean (*Erythrina flabeliformis*), ocotillo (*Fouquieria splendens*), mesquite (*Prosopis juliflora*, shrubform or tree), wait-a-minute bush (*Mimosa biuncifera*), Wislizenius dalea (*Dalea wislizeni*), feather dalea (*Dalea formosa*), turpentine bush (*Aplopappus laricifolius*), sotol (*Dasylirion wheeleri*), Thornber yucca (*Yucca baccata thornberi*), and palmilla (*Yucca elata*).

The cacti here include woodland and forest subspecies of the pincushion (*Mammillaria vivipara*), cream cactus (*Mammillaria heyderi*), and hedgehog (*Echinocereus troglichidiatus*), as well as species from the desert and grassland such as sahuaro (*Cereus giganteus*), tree cholla (*Opuntia versicolor*), and Wislizenius barrel cactus (*Echinocactus wislizeni*) which are occasional along the lower edge of the woodland; prickly pear cactus is often present. Conspicuous perennial herbs include species of beardtongue (*Penstemon*), verbena (*Verbena*), globemallow (*Sphaeralcea*), lupine (*Lupinus*), mint (*Salvia*), mariposa (*Calochortus*), et. al.

A few grasses, such as bullgrass (*Muhlenbergia emersleyi*), little bluestem (*Andropogon scoparius*), and wooly bunchgrass (*Elyonurus barbiculmus*), center in the southerly woodland habitats. Others, such as wolftail (*Lycurus phleoides*) and plains lovegrass (*Eragrostis intermedia*), occur principally in woodland, chaparral, and in the upper parts of desert-grassland. Most of the grasses in the southwestern woodlands, however, are species primarily of the grassland or, less commonly, of the forest;

Fig. 36. Oak-pine Woodland. Upper Sonoran. South side Santa Catalina Mountains, 6,000 ft. The tall pine at left-center is Chihuahua pine (*Pinus leiophylla chihuahuana*). The silhouetted tree with rounded crown at right-center is alligator juniper. The oaks are primarily silverleaf oak (*Quercus hypoleucoides*). A few ponderosa pines (upper right) occur at this elevation which is near the lower edge of the forest. Photo by Forrest Shreve.

blue grama (*Bouteloua gracilis*) is the most common grass throughout the evergreen woodland formation in Arizona.

Small stands of Arizona cypress (*Cupressus arizonica*) occur sporadically and primarily at mid-elevations in the evergreen woodland of mountains in southern Arizona, between 3,500 and 7,200 feet elevation. These relictual (post-climax) pockets, which often contain cypress trees up to 70 feet in height, are all restricted to north-facing slopes and/or canyon bottoms where soil moisture is relatively high and the temperatures in both summer and winter are moderate (Fig. 37). The subspecies *Cupressus arizonica arizonica* occurs from northern Mexico to mountains in southern Arizona which are mostly south of the Gila River (in Pima, Cochise, Graham, and Greenlee Counties). The contiguous subspecies *C. a. glabra* occurs between the Gila River and the Mogollon Rim (Coconino County and the adjacent northern parts of Maricopa and Gila Counties).

Precipitation in woodland habitats in southern Arizona is bi-seasonal and usually somewhat greater in summer than in winter, with annual rainfall usually between 12 and 22 inches; winter precipitation is predominantly in the form of rain rather than snow. The essentially Sierra Madrean characteristic of these woodlands is importantly determined both by the quite moderate minimum winter temperatures which ordinarily prevail, and by the southwestern summer monsoon with its principal rainfall during warm July-August.

Northern Arizona. In northern Arizona where minimum winter temperatures are markedly lower and summer temperatures are also lower, the woodland is composed essentially of junipers and pinyons (Fig. 38, 39). Annual precipitation varies from 12 to 20 inches and in winter it is predominantly in the form of snow. *Juniper-pinyon woodland* covers large areas below ponderosa pine forest on (and near) the Mogollon, Coconino, and Kaibab plateaus, most characteristically between 5,500 and 7,000 feet, and it covers the often flat-topped mesas and plateaus of Navajo and Apache Counties between 5,800 and 7,200 feet elevation. It is also present in several other northern areas including parts of the Strip Country north and west of the Grand Canyon. The woodlands as a whole are among the simplest vegetations in the Southwest, as far as dominant plants are concerned, and juniper-pinyon is perhaps the simplest of the woodlands. Below 6,500-6,800 feet the junipers are more abundant than the pinyons and may occur in pure stands, often as a juniper-grass "savanna." More or less dense stands of juniper (juniper woodland), and open stands of juniper (juniper grassland), occur as minor associations in both northern and southern Arizona (*e.g.,* Pima and Santa Cruz Counties) below 6,500 feet. Above this elevation the pinyons reach their greatest size and they also sometimes grow in large pure stands. By and large, in Arizona as elsewhere in the Southwest, junipers are generally more prevalent and more important in making up the juniper-pinyon woodland matrix than is pinyon (Woodin and Lindsey, 1954).

Colorado pinyon (*Pinus edulis*) is the common and characteristic species of pinyon almost throughout, and Utah juniper (*Juniperus osteosperma*) and one-seed juniper (*J. monosperma*) are the common and widespread junipers. Singleleaf pinyon (*Pinus monophylla*) occurs locally with Utah juniper, mostly in the northwestern corner of the state. Rocky

Fig. 37. Arizona Cypress in the evergreen woodland. Upper Sonoran. An essentially pure stand. Bear Canyon, 5,450 ft., north-facing slope in Santa Catalina Mountains. This beautiful tree (*Cypressus arizonica*) occurs in relict stands (postclimax) now restricted to north-facing slopes and riparian habitats at mid-elevations in Sub-Mogollon evergreen woodlands. Greater stature (to 90 feet) is obtained by those growing in canyon bottoms.

Fig. 38. Juniper-pinyon Woodland. Upper Sonoran. Utah juniper (*J. osteosperma*) and pinyon (*Pinus edulis*) in Skull Valley, Yavapai County. A common feature of juniper-pinyon woodland is simple structural and floristic composition, usually with a "ground cover" essentially of grass as shown here, or a simple shrub understory such as sagebrush (*Artemisia*). Photo by Robert R. Humphrey.

Mountain juniper (*J. scopulorum*) is scattered primarily in the northeast. Alligator juniper[19] and Mexican pinyon, which are the species commonly occurring with evergreen oaks in the mountains of the south, are absent in the north; alligator juniper still occurs today in the central part of the state. It is well known that juniper, as well as mesquite and other southwestern trees, have widely extended onto some of Arizona's former range grasslands (Miller, 1921; Pearson, 1931; Parker, 1945; Arnold and Schroeder, 1955; Humphrey, 1962; and others).

Grasses are (or were) more or less abundant throughout juniper-pinyon woodland. The predominant species include blue grama (one of

[19] In addition to alligator juniper (*J. deppeana pachyphlea*), one-seed juniper (*J. monosperma*) of the north is occasionally present in southern Arizona, in the edge of the desert-grassland and lower edge of the woodland (not in mountains) in Cochise County and western Pima and Santa Cruz Counties.

Fig. 39. Juniper-pinyon Woodland and Great Basin Desertscrub. Upper Sonoran. Looking northeast from west of Cameron, Coconino County, across Little Colorado River Gorge, and across the "Painted Desert" to its bordering plateaus ("the Hopi Mesas"). The "Painted Desert," which lies essentially below 5,000 feet elevation, comprises a relatively small area within the Great Basin Desert. Elevation of juniper-pinyon woodland in foreground approximately 6,000 ft. Photo by E. Tad Nichols.

the most important), sideoats grama, black grama, Arizona fescue, pinyon ricegrass, junegrass, indian ricegrass, needlegrass, sand dropseed, squirreltail, and ring-grass. Commonly a grass such as blue gamma (*Bouteloua gracilis*) or Arizona fescue (*Festuca arizonica*) is the most abundant herbaceous plant present in the stand. The more conspicuous herbs include species of globemallow, beardtongue, mariposa, paintbrush, *et al.*

59

While the understory shrubs are varied and often numerous (or, indeed, quite sparse and scattered), the dry-tropic species that are so characteristic of the southern oak type woodlands are either entirely absent or weakly represented in the northern woodlands of the state. Characteristic understory shrubs in the juniper-pinyon woodland of central and northern Arizona include cliffrose (*Cowania mexicana*), big sagebrush (*Artemisia tridentata*), serviceberry (*Amelanchier alnifolia*), rabbitbrush (*Chrysothamnus nauseosus, C. depressus*), fernbush (*Chamaebatiaria millifolium*), Navajo ephedra (*Ephedra viridis*), Fremont barberry (*Berberis fremonti*), Apache-plume (*Fallugia paradoxa*), antelope-brush (*Purshia tridentata*), black sage (*Artemisia nova*), banana yucca (*Yucca baccata*), Whipple cholla (*Opuntia whipplei*), beavertail (*O. basilaris*), fragile cholla (*O. fragilis*), prickly pear (*O. polyacantha*), and red hedgehog cactus (*Echinocereus triglochidiatus melanacanthus*).

One or more of the distinctly Great Basin desert species such as big sagebrush (*Artemisia tridentata*), shadscale (*Atriplex confertifolia*), blackbrush (*Coleogyne ramosissima*), and winterfat (*Eurotia lanata*), occur in the lower portion of the woodland; big sagebrush, moreover, occurs throughout approximately the elevational range of this woodland in Arizona. Chaparral forms such as silktassel (*Garrya wrighti*), mountain-mahogany (*Cerocarpus intricatus, C. ledifolius*), scrub oak (*Quercus turbinella*) and Gambel oak (*Q. gambeli*, in thicket shrubform) are commonly present, and species of the ponderosa pine forest such as buckbrush (*Ceanothus fendleri*) and pine cactus (*Opuntia erinacea xanthostema*) occur in the upper part of the woodland.

Deciduous (Riparian) Woodland

The deciduous woodlands are *riparian woodlands,* i.e., they occur along streams, rivers, floodplains and the like. They are comprised mostly of broadleaf trees which are winter deciduous, such as cottonwood, willow, and walnut (Fig. 40, 41, 65, 66). The species and/or genera are several friends in "the woods at home" of the eastern United States. Both their distinctive life-form and their riparian habitat distinguish these woodlands immediately from the evergreen western woodlands. The associated animals are conspicuously different in the two biotic communities, although the one (riparian) may course, finger-like, through the other. Zonally the habitat extends from the Lower Sonoran into Canadian, rarely into the Hudsonian zone.

The trees are often large, some species reaching heights of 50 to 100 feet (*e.g.*, cottonwood, sycamore, and alder). Thus the woodland may be a fairly high-canopied gallery association. Excluded from this formation are low shrubby stream thickets without trees, mountain meadows, and aspen (or maple, or other tree) stands or thickets which occur on slopes without immediate stream development.

Fig. 40. Riparian Woodland. Upper Sonoran. The cottonwood-willow gallery association of broadleaf, winter deciduous trees on Sonoita Creek, 4,000 ft., just west of Patagonia, Santa Cruz County. Mesquites may form an intermittent lower story on the stream bank beneath the broadleaf canopy (center-right), as well as forming extensive "mesquite bosques" on the adjacent flood plains. The surrounding terrain is desert-grassland and oak woodland. The stream is permanent and supports five species of native fishes and some introduced panfishes. Photo by E. Tad Nichols.

This is the least xeric of the woodlands, and one of the most mesic of all the strictly terrestrial ecologic formations in the Southwest. The habitat is in and along the channels, their margins, and/or floodplains of the larger and/or better watered drainageways. In southern Arizona most of these drainageways are the permanent and intermittent streamways of the conifer-clad mountains and their arroyo extensions into rivers and river beds which may still receive a sufficient flow above or below ground surface.

The species composition changes with elevation. Riparian woodland distributed along major drainageways throughout the evergreen woodlands and much of the conifer forests is characterized by such deciduous broadleaf trees as Texas mulberry (*Morus microphylla*), Arizona alder (*Alnus oblongifolia*), narrowleaf cottonwood (*Populus angustifolia*), southwestern chokecherry (*Prunus serotina virens*), boxelder (*Acer negundo*), Rocky Mountain maple (*Acer glabrum*), and Scouler willow (*Salix scouleriana*).

Within the broadleaf riparian woodland, isolated oak trees (*e.g.*, *Q. emoryi, Q. arizonica, Q. oblongifolia, Q. hypoleucoides*) occasionally finger down into the desert as far as 1,000 feet below the oak zone, and scrub oak to an elevation of 2,500 feet or lower (*e.g., Q. turbinella ajoensis*). Mesquite (*Prosopis juliflora*), catclaw (*Acacia greggi*) and others, often form a distinctive microphyllous border association on adjacent floodplains.

In the center of the Sub-Mogollon region, the riparian "big-five" are cottonwood (*Populus fremonti*), willow (*Salix bonplandiana* and others), sycamore (*Platanus wrighti*), ash (*Fraxinus pennsylvanica velutina*, and others), and walnut (*Juglans major*). Often three or four of these species may occur together, and occasionally all five. All of them are large, winter-deciduous broadleaf trees of genera and families different from those of the immediately bordering non-riparian climax desert or grassland communities. (Fig. 41).

This broadleaf association forms the conspicuous and dominant plant component of a biotic community which includes characteristic species of aquatic, and semi-aquatic, and terrestrial animals. Examples of these are the summer tanager (*Piranga rubra*), Bullock oriole (*Icterus bullocki*), yellow warbler (*Dendroica petechia*), Sonoran mud turtle (*Kinosternon sonoriense*), black-necked garter snake (*Thamnophis cyrtopsis*), leopard frog (*Rana pipiens*), canyon treefrog (*Hyla arenicolor*), longfin dace (*Agosia chrysogaster*), other vertebrates, and a larger number of invertebrates.

A riparian association of any kind is one which occurs in or adjacent to drainageways and/or their floodplains and which is further characterized by species and/or life-forms different from that of the immediately surrounding non-riparian climax. The southwestern riparian woodland formation is characterized by a complex of trees, and their plant and animal associates, restricted to the major drainageways that transgress the landscape of desert upward into forest. It is incorrect to regard this biotic formation as merely a temporary unstable, seral community. It is an evolutionary entity with an enduring stability equivalent to that of the landscape drainageways which form its physical habitat. That is, it is a distinctive climax biotic community. Moreover, it is, as are all ecologic formations and their subdivisions, locally subject to, and often dissolved by, the vicissitudes of human occupation. In Arizona, the riparian woodlands have been rapidly dwindling just as the water table has been rapidly lowering. And its trees are now the native phraeatophytes of the water-users.

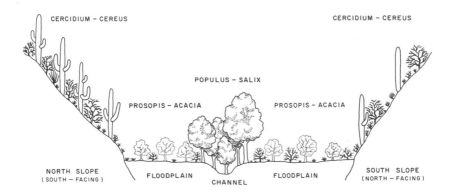

Fig. 41. Diagrammatic profile of a foothill canyon in the Sonoran Desert, as in the Galiuro and Santa Catalina Mountains at approximately 3,000 feet elevation. Stream-flow is either permanent or semi-permanent and in either case periodically torrential. The riparian woodland of cottonwood, willow, ash, sycamore, and walnut (cotton-wood-willow gallery association) is situated in and at the immediate edge of the channel. This broadleaf deciduous woodland is immediately bordered by a mesquite dominated floodplain characterized by deciduous microphylls (*Prosopis-Acacia* flood-plain community). The non-riparian climax on the adjoining slopes is paloverde desert-scrub (*Cercidium-Cereus* upland community) dominated primarily by aphyllous and microphyllous deciduous and often spinose life-forms of trees, shrubs, and cacti.

Transition Life-zone

The Transition Zone is equivalent to *pine forest*, and specifically to *ponderosa pine forest* (western yellow pine forest). Thus the entire zone in Arizona, and often elsewhere, is the *association* and also frequently the *consociation* (pure stand) dominated by the single species *Pinus ponderosa*. Mature trees reach large size (to 125 feet), are commonly 200 to 400 years old, and may exceed 500 years in age.

Elevation of the forest is ordinarily between 6,000 and 9,000 feet; 6,000-7,000 feet at the lower extreme, and 8,500-9,000 feet at the higher, varying according to slope exposure. Pure stands of ponderosa, however, occur most commonly between 7,000 and 8,000 feet. The lower limit of the ponderosa pine forest is the lower elevational limit of the entire coniferous forest formation within Arizona. This lower ecologic limit is controlled by several factors of which critical low level of plant-avail-able soil moisture is the primary direct factor (Shreve, 1915; Sampson, 1918; Pearson, 1920, 1931; Daubenmire, 1943a). Precipitation within this zone is approximately 18 to 26 inches annually; rarely lower.

Fig. 42. Ponderosa Pine Forest. Transition. View from Sunset Crater toward east face of San Francisco Mountain (San Francisco Peaks) across part of volcanic field of same name, 7,000 ft. In the foreground is the cinder-covered Bonita lava flow which emerged from the base of Sunset Crater and which has remained largely unforested. It is early summer and patches of snow remain on the high peaks bordering the Inner Basin of this old volcano which once stood about 3,000 feet higher than at present—12,670 feet on Humphreys Peak (right center). Photo by E. Tad Nichols.

This is a major forest type that covers much of the Kaibab Plateau and Mogollon Mesa, and other areas on the extensive Colorado Plateau (Fig. 42, 43); Rocky Mountain ponderosa pine (*Pinus ponderosa scopulorum* Engelm.) is the subspecies in this area. Transition is also the principal (largest area) forest life-zone on the higher conifer-clad mountains of the state, including several of the desert-border ("desert") mountains located south of the Salt River (Fig. 44, 45). Arizona ponderosa pine (*Pinus ponderosa arizonica* Engelm.) is the primary subspecies (typically 5-needled) in the southern area (primarily in Pima, Santa Cruz, and Cochise counties).[20] In addition to the different tree subspecies which occur, there are several

[20] Subspecies (subsp.) of plants may still be referred to as varieties (var.) in some references. Some mountains in southern Arizona, such as the Santa Catalinas near Tucson, have two subspecies of ponderosa pine: one (*P. p. scopulorum*) at the higher elevations mostly above 8,000 feet elevation on south-facing slopes, and the other (*P. p. arizonica*) at lower elevations mostly between 6,000 and 8,000 feet.

Fig. 43. Ponderosa Pine Forest. Transition. Navajo · County. This is a landscape characteristic of the ponderosa forest across *central and northern* Arizona on flat and gently rolling plateau country; grass is the principal "ground cover." The relatively open, park-like stand across more or less level expanses is a feature almost entirely lacking in the forested mountains of *southern* Arizona where, in sharp contrast, the gradients are steep, soils more shallow, and shrubs more common. Photo by Robert R. Humphrey.

notable differences between the Transition Zone habitats of the southern mountains south of the Salt River and those to the north, on the Colorado Plateau.

Southern Arizona. The southern conifer-clad mountains, such as the Pinals, Gilas, Pinalenos, Galiuros, Santa Catalinas, Santa Ritas, Huachucas, and Chiricahuas, are isolated ranges[21] with relatively steep topography when compared to the extensive mesas and plateaus to the north. There are few level areas with parks or mountain meadows. Flood plains are small and not well developed, for typically the streams are narrowly confined and their gradients are steep.

These rugged ranges are populated with many species of plants and animals that have their areas of principal distribution in Mexico and

---

[21] "Sky islands" (Heald, 1951), seems to me quite apt. They are often called "desert mountains" or "desert mountain islands" which are inappropriate, for they are not surrounded by desert. They are bordered on one or more sides by grassland as well as by desertscrub on the other sides.

Fig. 44. Ponderosa Pine Forest. Transition. Ponderosa pine (*Pinus ponderosa arizonica*) in the *lower* part of the forest, 7,000 ft., Santa Catalina Mountains, Pima County. Silverleaf oak (*Quercus hypoleucoides*) is the characteristic broadleaf tree. Madrone (*Arbutus arizonica*) and netleaf oak (*Q. rugosa*) are also present along with alligator juniper and Chihuahua pine, all evergreen. Photo by Forrest Shreve.

reach their northern limits in Arizona below and south of the Mogollon Rim. At lower elevations, silverleaf oak (*Quercus hypoleucoides*), netleaf oak (*Quercus reticulata*), and madroño (*Arbutus arizonica*) are usually the commonest broadleaf evergreen trees. At higher elevations, and in cooler and more mesic situations, Gambel oak (*Quercus gambeli*), bigtooth maple (*Acer grandidentatum*), aspen (*Populus tremuloides*), alder (*Alnus oblongifolia*), and mulberry (*Morus microphylla*) are common broadleaf deciduous trees. Similarly, among the coniferous associates, Chihuahua pines are occasionally scattered among the ponderosa pines at the lower zone limit and alligator juniper is scattered throughout the lower, more xeric parts of the zone, while Douglas fir (*Pseudotsuga menziesi*) and white pine (*Pinus ayacahuite*) become fairly frequent in the upper and more mesic parts. In these ranges, ponderosa parklands with well-developed grass areas and/or shrub understories, so typical in the north, are more often virtually non-existent.

Buckbrush (*Ceanothus fendleri*) is the small shrub that is prominent throughout the southern pine forest to about 9,000 feet; it may be the only shrub present on the forest floor, and may form thickets on slopes

Fig. 45. Ponderosa Pine Forest. Transition. Typical dense stand in the *upper* part of the forest, between 8,000 and 9,000 ft., Santa Catalina Mountains. In addition to dominant ponderosa pine (*Pinus ponderosa scopulorum*), white pine (*Pinus ayacahuite*) and Douglas fir (*Pseudotsuga menziesi*) are present. The deciduous Gambel oak (*Quercus gambeli*) is a characteristic broadleaf tree, and evergreen oaks (silverleaf and netleaf) are also present; but neither alligator juniper, pinyon, nor Chihuahua pine reach 8,000 ft. elevation. Photo by Forrest Shreve (1915, plate 35).

where the forest is particularly open. Boxleaf myrtle (*Pachystima myrsinites*) is a low, creeping, inconspicuous undershrub that is more commonly seen in the upper part of the forest. Arizona rose (*Rosa arizonica*) along streams, and New Mexican locust (*Robinia neomexicana*) as a large and conspicuous shrub or small tree occur throughout much of the forest. Between 8,500 and 9,000 feet, snowberry (*Symphoricarpos oreophilus*), ocean spray (*Holodiscus dumosus*), orange gooseberry (*Ribes pinetorum*), and other shrubs which are also common to fir forest and spruce-fir forest, enter the upper portion of ponderosa pine forest.

In the lower part of the forest, shrubs of the woodland or chaparral are often present, such as buckthorn (*Rhamnus crocea, R. betulaefolia, R. californica*), deerbrush (*Ceanothus integerrimus*), manzanita (*Arctostaphylos pungens, A. pringlei*), squawbush (*Rhus trilobata*), silktassel (*Garrya wrighti*), mountain yucca (*Yucca schotti*), and hedgehog cactus (*Echinocereus triglochidiatus*). Scarlet sumac (*Rhus glabra*) occasionally forms thickets in the lower edge of the forest. Also here, two of the prominent oaks of the pine forest (the facultative species *Q. hypoleucoides* and *Q. reticulata*) may be in shrub form rather than tree form, and western chokecherry (*Prunus serotina*) also may be a shrub or small tree.

In many of the genera of perennial herbs common to the southern and northern ponderosa pine forests in Arizona and New Mexico, the species and/or subspecies may be different; for example, as in lupine (*Lupine*), peavine (*Lathyrus*), cinquefoil (*Potentilla*), yarrow (*Achillea*), goldenrod (*Solidago*), paintbrush (*Castilleja*), beardtongue (*Penstemon*), fleabane (*Erigeron*), deervetch (*Lotus*), groundsel (*Senecio*), pinque (*Actinea*), milkvetch (*Astragalus*), violet (*Viola*), and many others. Conversely, many of them which occur in the two forest areas are of the same species; for example, bracken fern (*Pteridium*), Fendler globemallow (*Sphaeralcea fendleri*), beebalm (*Monarda*), flag (*Iris*), mullein (*Verbascum*, introduced), toadflax (*Commandra*), mock-pennyroyal (*Hedeoma*), golden pea (*Thermopsis*), and other species of lupine, yarrow, *et al.*

The most characteristic grasses are the two mountain muhlys (*Muhlenbergia montana, M. virescens*). Other characteristic grasses are pine dropseed (*Blepharoneuron tricholepis*) and pinyon ricegrass (*Piptochaetium fimbriatum*). Most of the characteristic grasses that are present in both the southern Arizona and northern Arizona pine forests are conspecific.

Northern and Central Arizona. In central and northern Arizona north of the Mogollon Rim, the ponderosa forests usually contain fewer trees of other species, but they are rich in shrubs and in the grass carpeting which often extends through park-like landscapes. On the few high mountains which rise abruptly from the Colorado Plateau in northern Arizona, *e.g.*, the San Francisco Mountains and Chuska Mountains, the Transition Zone of ponderosa pine forest is also present on rugged precipitous terrain as it is on the mountains in the Basin and Range Province in southern Arizona. Such is not the usual situation, however, for, as already noted, Transition Zone in northern Arizona is typically distributed over very extensive areas of flat to rolling plateau country.

Gambel oak is the most common tree associated with the pines, and quaking aspen may be scattered or may be in large stands on old burns, usually above 7,500 feet. In the lower part of the zone, below 7,000-7,500 feet, pinyon, juniper, and big sagebrush may be mingled with the pines; Douglas fir is occasional to frequent above about 7,000 feet.

Understory shrubs, in climax stands, may be essentially lacking to fairly common though more or less widely and irregularly spaced. Also, some shrubs (*e.g.*, species of *Artemisia*) may be locally abundant, particularly at lower elevations in the forest as seen on the South Rim of Grand Canyon and in the Navajo Indian Reservation where ponderosa pine occurs. And other shrubs (*Ceanothus, Berberis*) may be more or less uniformly distributed over large areas.

Among the most characteristic shrubs of this northern Arizona forest are buckbrush (*Ceanothus fendleri*), fernbush (*Chamaebatiaria millefolium*), Gambel oak (*Quercus gambeli*, shrubform), fendlerella (*Fendlerella utahensis*), wax currant (*Ribes cereum*), New Mexican locust (*Robinia neomexicana*), Canadian elder (*Sambucus coerulea*), greenleaf manzanita (*Arctostaphylos patula*), Parry rabbitbrush (*Chrysothamnus parryi*), big sagebrush (*Artemisia tridentata*), black sagebrush (*A. nova*), cliffrose (*Cowania mexicana*), Apache-plume (*Fallugia paradoxa*), and mockorange (*Philadelphus microphyllus*). At higher elevations the shrubs of the pine forest are more commonly species shared with the fir forest and spruce-alpine fir forest: ninebark (*Physocarpus monogynus*), raspberry (*Rubus strigosus*), shrubby dwarf juniper (*Juniperus communis montana*), ocean spray (*Holodiscus dumosus glabrescens*), Oregon grape (*Berberis repens*), cliffbush (*Jamesia americana*) and boxleaf myrtle (*Pachystima myrsinites*).

Grasses characteristic of the northern Arizona ponderosa forests include Arizona fescue, mountain muhly, pine dropseed, squirreltail, mountain brome, spike muhly, deer grass, junegrass, and bluestem; blue grama is common in forest openings. Perennial herbs (root perennials) in addition to those already noted in the discussion of the understory plants in the southern Arizona ponderosa forests are meadowrue (*Thalictrum fendleri*), vetch (*Vicia americana*), locoweed (*Oxytropis lamberti*), and sage (*Artemisia ludoviciana*). These are typical pine forest associates more or less throughout the state.

Canadian Life-zone

The Canadian Zone is equivalent to *fir forest*, i.e., *Douglas fir forest*. Elevation is from about 7,500-8,000 to 9,000-9,500 feet (according to slope exposure), and occasionally the zone extends to higher elevations of nearly 10,000 feet. Precipitation is approximately 25 to 30 inches annually.

The fir forest stands are typically of mixed species rather than of a single species as is much of the ponderosa pine forest. Douglas fir (*Pseudotsuga menziesi*) and white fir (*Abies concolor*) are the principal trees (Fig. 46, 47). Douglas fir has the wider tolerance, extends to lower elevation, and predominates on south-facing exposures; white fir may predominate on northerly exposures. Both trees reach large size (about 150 ft. ht.) and stands are commonly 200 to 400 years of age. At the higher elevations, alpine fir (*Abies lasiocarpa*) may be present, and white pines are occasional to frequent; the species in northern Arizona is limber pine (*Pinus flexilis*), and in the southwestern mountains it is southwestern white pine (*Pinus ayacahuite*).

Ponderosa pine may be present, but more or less confined to ridges and southerly exposures except along the lower edge of the fir forest where the two forests tend to merge in the continuum. There are physiographic, ecologic, and taxonomic differences between the fir (Canadian) forests of

Fig. 46. Fir Forest. Canadian. North slopes of Mount Lemmon, Santa Catalina Mountains, 8,700 ft. The trees are white fir (*Abies concolor*), Douglas fir (*Pseudotsuga menziesi*) and white pine (*Pinus ayacahuite*). The slope is gentle at this site but shortly becomes steep as is commonly the case throughout the forest on the mountains of southern Arizona. Photo by Forrest Shreve (1915, plate 1).

northern Arizona and those of southern Arizona which are similar to those already noted for the Transition Zone (ponderosa pine).

Gambel oak (*Q. gambeli*), box elder (*Acer negundo*), water birch (*Betula occidentalis*), and blueberry elder (*Sambucus glauca*), are among the conspicuous broadleaf deciduous trees, as are Rocky Mountain maple at higher elevations and locust at lower elevations. Quaking aspen (*Populus tremuloides*) forms a successional subclimax community (following burns and other disturbances in the forest) that is particularly well developed and conspicuous in this zone prior to re-establishment of the coniferous forest which follows the aspens in time (Fig. 48); this is also true in the Hudsonian Zone and in the upper part of the Transition Zone.

There are few (if any) distinctive understory species either on the floor of the fir forest or on the stream banks and flood plains. In dense stands a considerable duff accumulates on the forest floor similar to that of spruce-fir forests. The shrubs, herbs, and grasses are usually species shared either with the pine forest below (such as bracken fern, vetch, and deers-ears) or spruce-alpine fir forest at higher elevations (such as wolf currant, owlclaws, and red elderberry). In the fir forest, sedges (*Carex*)

Fig. 47. Fir Forest. Canadian. An alluvial flat in fir forest, north slope of Mount Lemmon, Santa Catalina Mountains, 8,600 ft. White fir (*Abies concolor*), ponderosa pine (*Pinus ponderosa*) and quaking aspen (*Populus tremuloides*). Photo by Forrest Shreve.

Fig. 48. Fir Forest. Canadian. Old stand of quaking aspen (*Populus tremuloides*), 9,000 ft., San Francisco Mountain. Note young conifers growing up under canopy of aspens in usual forest succession. Photo by E. Tad Nichols.

become conspicuous and there is no longer evidence of the dry-tropic species of trees, shrubs, succulents, and cacti which enter from below and partly traverse the floor of the yellow pine forest; this is equally true in Sub-Mogollon southern Arizona as well as north of the Mogollon Rim.

The Canadian Zone reaches its greatest development in Arizona on the higher ranges rising from the Colorado Plateau in the central, northern, and eastern parts of the state, and there one of its best developments is in the extensive elevated mass called the White Mountains, southwest of Springerville (Fig. 52). It is occasionally well developed as a forest stand or zone on the higher mountains in the southern part of the state, e.g., on the Santa Catalinas, Santa Ritas, Huachucas, Chiricahuas, and Pinalenos (Fig. 46). Throughout the state, fir forest occurs where it is with few exceptions situated in rugged terrain, and is rarely seen on broad plateaus and flat mesas as is characteristic of ponderosa pine forest in central and northern Arizona.

On the high mountains which "top out" at about 9,000 feet elevation in southern Arizona and in adjacent parts of neighboring states, the fir forest is usually present without spruce-alpine fir forest above it.[22] On such mountains, the fir forest is very distinctive (Fig. 46). It extends downward on the north-facing slopes from the summit to about 7,500 feet elevation, the lower limit varying somewhat with latitude, base-level elevation, mountain mass, etc. The south-facing slopes are covered with ponderosa pine forest. Northward in central and northern Arizona on the Colorado Plateau, however, the fir forest (Canadian Zone) often has a wavering sort of existence intermingled more or less with the spruce-alpine fir forest. As a result of this situation on the Colorado Plateau north of the Mogollon Rim in Arizona and New Mexico, the forest types (Douglas fir-white fir, and spruce-alpine fir) have been considered together as the Northern Mesic Evergreen Forest (Shreve, 1942, Arizona), Petran Subalpine Forest (Castetter, 1956, New Mexico), Boreal Forest, etc.

The environmental tolerances and hence the ecologic and geographic distributions of spruces, firs, Douglas fir, and white pines widely overlap in the Rocky Mountain region. It is not surprising, therefore, that the two mesic forest types in Arizona are not always easily distinguishable in some areas, and that they tend on the whole to contain similar groups of species. Somewhat greater differences are seen in the herb, grass, and sedge components of the two forests.

---

[22] South of the Gila River in Arizona, only two mountain ranges contain spruce (*Picea engelmanni*) in their floras. These are the Pinaleno and the Chiricahua Mountains. The former exceeds and the latter closely approaches 10,000 feet elevation. The spruce stands on the Chiricahuas, in Cochise County, were thought to be the southernmost in North America. Engelmann spruce, however, is reported from the northern part of the Sierra Madre in Chihuahua, Mexico.

Hudsonian Life-zone

The Hudsonian Zone is equivalent to *spruce-alpine fir forest* (Fig. 49, 50). It occurs around and on the summits of the highest ranges, such as the Chiricahua Mountains, Graham Mountains, White Mountains, San Francisco Mountains (summit is alpine tundra), and on the large summit area of the Kaibab Plateau. Elevation is from approximately 8,500 to 9,000 feet at the lower limit to approximately 11,500 feet maximum elevation; precipitation is approximately 30 to 35 inches per annum.

The primary trees are Engelmann spruce, blue spruce, alpine fir (corkbark fir), limber pine, and bristlecone pine (also called foxtail pine). Rocky Mountain maple (*Acer glabrum*), bitter cherry (*Prunus emarginata*), Bebb willow (*Salix bebbiana*), Scouler willow (*Salix scouleriana*), and thin-leaf alder (*Alnus tenufolia*) are among the broadleaf deciduous trees which may be present where the forest is not with completely closed canopy. Aspen occurs as scattered trees, small clumps, or in large and often pure (subclimax) stands.

Engelmann spruce (*Picea engelmanni*) is the principal dominant of the spruce-alpine fir forest, and alpine fir (*Abies lasiocarpa*) is the usually common, characteristic fir tree that is a remarkably constant companion; cornbark fir (*A. l. arizonica*) is a subspecies (variety) of alpine fir occurring in the southern Rocky Mountains, from Colorado to Arizona. Climax spruce-alpine fir forest reaches 80 or more feet in height, varying according to closeness of the trees and other factors. Pure Engelmann spruce stands may well exceed 250 years of age, while alpine fir is a shorter-lived species that tends to die out in old forest stands.

Blue spruce (*Picea glauca*) is a major dominant on the extensive summit area of the Kaibab Plateau, an area which is essentially spruce-fir forest with interspersed mountain grassland (Fig. 49). It is absent from the forests of southern Arizona. Bristlecone pine (*Pinus aristata*) is a conspicuous tree in the upper part of the spruce-fir forest on high San Francisco Mountain, near Flagstaff, and is one of the two gnarled conifers (Engelmann spruce and bristlecone pine) in the prostrate wind-timber (Krummholz) there at timberline (see Arctic-Alpine Zone below).

As noted earlier, the two primary conifers of the Canadian Zone (Douglas fir and white fir) may be present with spruce, and occasionally extensively so, as on Mount Thomas (Baldy Peak) and other areas in the White Mountains, and on the Kaibab Plateau. White pine is also widely distributed in both life-zones and also occurs (but to a much more limited extent) in the upper part of the Transition Zone.

At high elevations on San Francisco Mountain, from above 9,000 to over 10,000 feet elevation, on the steep slopes with well-marked north and south exposures, Engelmann spruce and alpine fir quite typically dominate the forest on northerly exposures all the way to timberline. But on south-facing slopes there is an equally striking forest type above the last Douglas

Fig. 49. Spruce-fir Forest. Hudsonian. Edge of forest on Kaibab Plateau, V T Park, north of Grand Canyon, 9,000 ft. The conifers are blue spruce (*Picea pungens*), the broadleaf trees aspen (*Populus tremuloides*). Blue spruce singularly dominates the forest bordering the mountain grassland, and elsewhere on south-facing slopes. Engelmann spruce (*P. engelmanni*) dominates in other areas on the Kaibab in which alpine fir (*Abies lasiocarpa*) is virtually absent, whereas white fir (*A. concolor*) and Douglas fir (*Pseudotsuga menziesi*) are conspicuously present.

firs that is dominated primarily by limber pine and/or bristlecone pine. This distinctive high pine association may be considered for present purposes a plant community (bristlecone pine-limber pine, *Pinus aristata-Pinus flexilis*) within the spruce-alpine fir biotic community; it usually has been so considered, when not merely ignored. In zonal terminology, bristlecone pine and limber pine form a high pine association in the Hudsonian Life-zone. However, I should point out that habitat-wise, the more open limber pine-bristlecone pine association is not merely intermediate between the climatic and edaphic conditions supporting fir forest and spruce-fir forest. Taken on the whole, such high limber pine forest is, in fact, very distinctive however small its total geographic extent in the Southwest (see Merriam, 1890; Pearson, 1931), and I have listed it in Tables 1 and 2.

Where the forest shade and litter may be reduced or absent — as along streamways, in natural forest openings, on old burns, and in trail cuts — a number of species of shrubs may occur as single plants or in small patches, or more rarely as rather extensive thickets. The characteristic shrubs are species of currant (*Ribes*), blueberry (*Vaccinium oreophyllum*), Oregon-grape (*Berberis repens*), black-fruited honeysuckle (*Lonicera involucrata*), dwarf juniper (*Juniperus communis montana*), red elderberry (*Sambucus racemosa*), and shrubby cinquefoil (*Potentilla fruticosa*). These occur also to either a lesser or greater extent in fir forest (Canadian Life-zone). Toward the upper limit, most of the shrubs have disappeared well before timberline is reached. However, two shrubs extend to and slightly beyond the timberline on San Francisco Mountain: dwarf juniper and gooseberry currant.

Herbs in the lower part of the Hudsonian again are species found also in the Canadian Zone; and the grasses present are mostly those in the Canadian Zone and the Transition Zone. However, the herbs, grasses, and sedges found in the higher parts of the spruce-alpine fir forest between 10,500 and 11,500 feet elevation are often species shared with the alpine tundra community and, in fact, are often primarily alpine tundra species. There are several sedges (*Carex*) and rushes (*Juncus*) and the grasses include mountain timothy (*Phleum alpinum*), red fescue (*Fescue rubra*) and spike trisetum (*Trisetum spicatum*).

Spruce-alpine fir communities are habitats for high elevation primroses (*Primula*), gentians (*Gentiana*), violets (*Viola*), columbines (*Aquilegia*) and other mountain favorites as well as skunk cabbage (*Veratrum*), owlclaws *Helenium*), baneberries (*Actaea*), louseworts (*Pedicularis*) and many others. Most of these herbaceous plants, however, are rare or totally absent in the shade of compact tree stands, as are the shrubs and grasses. In the shade of such climax overstories a heavy duff usually accumulates on the forest floor; sedges, mosses, liverworts and lichens are the characteristic plants and they may be locally abundant.

On San Francisco Mountain where highest Humphreys Peak is 12,670 feet, the Hudsonian Zone timberline varies from about 11,000 feet on northerly slopes to 11,400-11,500 feet on southerly exposures. Slope exposure, toward or away from the sun, is the most important local condition producing the 400-500 foot variation in this upper limit for forest tree growth. Spruce-alpine -fir forest occurs with no true alpine

Fig. 50. Spruce-fir Forest. Hudsonian. Rockslide at 11,000 ft. on old Weatherford Road, north slope Fremont Peak, San Francisco Mountain. The trees are Englemann spruce and young ones have established on the old road cut without succession preceded by aspen or other trees. Quaking aspen does not reach this elevation on north-facing slopes, although it occasionally does on south-facing slopes. Photo by H. K. Gloyd.

timberline (Krummholz) at the summit area of Baldy Peak in the White Mountains, although, as noted, conditions there approach timberline.

Arctic-Alpine Life-zone

The Arctic-Alpine Zone is represented in Arizona by a summit area of alpine tundra, an "arctic" type vegetation, isolated on the top of San Francisco Mountain (to 12,670 feet) above its timberline (Fig. 51). This is the only true Arctic-Alpine in Arizona, although tree stature beginning to approach timberline conditions can be seen in the White Mountains (Arizona's second highest) on Baldy Peak (11,470 feet) which is forested to the summit by conifers, and on Mount Graham (10,713 feet) in the Pinaleno (Graham) Mountains south of the Gila River in Graham County.

Geography and geology of the San Francisco Mountain region are given by Robinson (1913), the alpine tundra climate by Merriam (1890), by Coville and MacDougal (1903), and by Pearson (1920, 1931), and the alpine tundra flora and vegetation by Merriam (1890) and by Little (1941).[23] The important paper by Elbert Little (1941) is the principal modern work on the alpine flora and vegetation of San Francisco Mountain.

[23] See also Hoffman (1877), Britton (1889), Rusby (1889), Harshberger (1911), Rydberg (1914), Holm (1927), Hesse, Allee and Schmidt (1937), Shreve (1942a), Daubenmire (1954), Castetter (1956), Billings and Bliss (1959), Fosberg (1959), Martin (1959), Webster (1961), and Beaman (1962).

Fig. 51. Alpine Tundra. Arctic-Alpine Life-zone. Humphreys Peak (12,670 ft.), San Francisco Mountain. Looking northwest across Inner Basin toward alpine tundra on Humphreys Peak, highest point in Arizona, from spruce-alpine fir forest on saddle of old Weatherford Road, *ca.* 11,000 ft., between Fremont Peak and Doyle Peak. Note the few lighter patches of quaking aspen among the conifers (Hudsonian Life-zone) on southeast-facing slope coming down to the inner basin. Trees in foreground at lower left are Engelmann spruce (*Picea engelmanni*).

San Francisco Mountain is about 10 miles north of Flagstaff, Coconino County. It is an eroded and truncated volcanic cone that earlier was about three thousand feet higher than it is now. Along the irregular crest line there are six peaks reaching above 11,000 feet elevation, and the mountain is known locally as the San Francisco Peaks. The three highest are Humphreys Peak (12,670 feet) on the northwest, Agassiz Peak (12,400 feet) on the southwest, and Fremont Peak (11,990 feet) on the south. One of the southernmost Pleistocene glaciers in the United States occupied the Inner Basin on the northeast side of the mountain, and was about two miles in length. The top of the mountain is about two miles in diameter and approximately a mile high, above its roughly 7,000-foot plateau base.

Elevation of the life-zone is from approximately 11,000 to 12,670 feet on Humphreys Peak and this is the alpine tundra community. Timberline is from approximately 11,000 to 11,400 feet, according to exposure. Precipitation is about 33 to 40 inches annually (it may well exceed 45 or 50 in any one year) and is distributed during both the cold and the warm seasons, but with relatively little occurring during the latter part of the growing season.

Fig. 51a. Alpine Tundra. Arctic-Alpine Life-zone. Easterly exposure below Humphreys Peak, *ca.* 11,600 ft., on the old Weatherford Trail, San Francisco Mountain, July 10, 1962; mid-July remnant of snow pack. Principal flowering herbs of foreground rock held are tundra daisies (*Erigeron simplex*) and gentians (*Gentiana* sp.). Small dwarfed trees appear as dark spots along ridge at upper left. Photo by R. R. Humphrey.

June to September is the usual growing season, with both the first frost and the first snowfall ordinarily occurring in early October. From November-December to March-April the mountain is snow-capped and patches of snow may remain into late August.

At timberline, the stunted and gnarled shrubby or prostrate Engelmann spruce and bristlecone pines grow singly or in scattered patches. Such patches may be found in alpine tundra beyond (above) the timberline tension zone (ecotone).[24] Two naturally shrubby species also occur here in the timberline transitional zone and just above it in wind-protected sites, *viz.*, gooseberry currant (*Ribes montigenum*) and dwarf juniper (*Juniperus communis montana*).

The complex of environmental determinants affecting the alpine timberline includes (1) strong ground wind forces and (2) winter low

---

[24] The "tree line" is theoretically that elevation of the last stunted tree, as distinguished from "forest line" which is the upper edge of the continuous forest.

temperature of air and soil, in relation to metabolism, photosynthesis, evapotranspiration, plant-available soil moisture, desiccation, wind shear, reproduction and cell death. Snow creep and avalanche, as well as tundra plant (sedge, genus *Carex*) competition, are additional known factors. Moreover, on the San Francisco Peaks above timberline the slopes are steep, rocky, and often covered with relatively loose volcanic debris. It is often difficult at best for trees to become established in such substratum conditions even without severe wind and frost action, and the treeline on the peaks is undoubtedly kept down at a somewhat lower elevation by the dual action of substratum and climate than it would be if it were a wholly climatic line (Brandegee, 1880; Merriam, 1899a; Shaw, 1909; Robinson, 1913; Adams, *et al.*, 1920; Forsaith, 1920; Pearson, 1920, 1931; Bates, 1924; Griggs, 1934, 1938, 1946; Shreve, 1942a; Daubenmire, 1943b; Raup, 1951).

Alpine tundra plants are uniformly small and low-growing, rarely more than a few inches above ground level, but many have large or showy flowers. Several are mat-forming cushion plants, and all are genetic dwarfs. Herbs, grasses, sedges, rushes, lichens, and mosses are characteristic; ferns and liverworts are also present. A remarkable number of the species in the flora are disjunctive from the high latitude tundra of Arctic North America and Eurasia; they range southward and eventually to the isolated high elevation alpine tundra in Arizona (San Francisco Mountain) and neighboring states, where these species reach their southernmost limits in North America. Twenty such species, roughly 40 per cent of the total of about 50, in the flora of the Arctic-Alpine Zone on San Francisco Mountain are such arctic-alpine disjuncts which also live in the arctic tundra. Fifteen of the twenty are circumpolar, *i.e.*, occurring in arctic Eurasia as well as in arctic North America. Two species appear to be endemic to San Francisco Mountain itself; a groundsel (*Senecio*) and a woodbetony (*Pedicularis*).

On the San Francisco Peaks only a few local areas above timberline are at all well covered with seed plants; this is largely a result of the steepness of the slope, looseness of soil, and presence of angular blocks and boulders. Some areas, such as unstable rock slides, are essentially without plants. The two primary tundra habitats and their plant associations are (1) the *alpine tundra rock field* (lichen association), and (2) the *alpine tundra meadow* (avens association). The two communities are often intermixed and many of the same species occur in both.

Alpine Tundra Rock Field. Crustose and foliose lichens occur on the rock surfaces, seed plants (herbs, grasses, sedges, rushes) are scattered between them, and mosses and ferns are found mostly in the rock crevices. The most abundant lichen is the crustose species *Rhizocarpon geographicum. Carex bella* is the common sedge, *Luzula spicata* (woodrush) the common rush, and the three grasses most commonly represented are alpine fescue (*Festuca ovina brachyphylla*), tundra bluegrass (*Poa rupi-*

cola), and spike trisetum (*Trisetum spicatum*). A single alpine fern, the bladder fern (*Crystopteris fragilis*) is commonly found in rock crevices. Most of the flowering plants above timberline are represented to some degree in this rock field habitat, including the most common of the species in the tundra meadow habitat (*Geum turbinatum* which is a mat-forming avens). The herbs of the rock field include several characteristic species which are arctic-alpine disjuncts, such as sandwort (*Arenaria sajanensis*), powderhorn (*Cerastium beeringianum*), moss campion (*Silene acaulis*), and Jacobs-ladder (*Polemonium confertum*).

Alpine Tundra Meadow. On San Francisco Mountain the alpine tundra meadows are not large nor particularly well-developed and they occupy but a small fraction of the Arctic-Alpine Zone. They are relatively "dry" and do not develop the "wet" meadow conditions as seen, for example, in the alpine tundra in the Colorado Rockies (Cox, 1933). The avens (*Geum turbinatum*) is the dominant plant, and other important mat-forming herbs include two arctic-alpine disjuncts, the circumpolar cinque-foil (*Potentilla sibbaldi*) and stemless catchfly (*Silene acaulis*). Two grasses essentially restricted to this association are mountain timothy *(Phleum alpinum)* and the bluegrass *Poa reflexa;* the other grasses listed above for rock fields are also present and are usually more abundant. In addition to the grasses, sedges (*Carex bella, C. albonigra, C. ebenea*) and rushes (*Luzula spicata, Juncus drummondi*) are, of course, typical of this association. Most of the herbs cited above for the alpine tundra rock fields are also present. In addition, there are a few herbs essentially restricted to the meadows and these include another arctic-alpine disjunct, the speedwell (*Veronica wormskjoldi*). Several species of mosses are present in the meadows, as is the one liverwort (*Lophozia porphyreleuca*) that is known from this zone on the mountain.

So it is, that in Arizona, isolated on high San Francisco Mountain above timberline, there live a number of circumpolar arctic-alpine plants that are widely distributed in arctic regions of the world such as Siberia, Alaska, and Greenland, and which extend southward on mountain tops of such impressive mountain ranges as the Himalayas, Alps, Sierra Nevada, and Rocky Mountains — and then reach the southern end of their distributions in North America on the high mountains of Arizona, California, and New Mexico.

With regard to the vertebrates, however, a single bird, the water pipit (*Anthus spinoletta alticola*) nests in the alpine tundra (meadow) on San Francisco Mountain,[25] and there are no mammals or other kinds of vertebrate animals represented (reproductively) there; man (*Homo sapiens*) is an occasional intruder. Three other birds which are well-known tundra species are represented in the faunas of New Mexico (white-

---

[25] The pipit also breeds in the alpine quasi-tundra on top of Baldy Peak (11,740 feet) in the White Mountains of Arizona, and in alpine tundra in New Mexico, but not in California.

tailed ptarmigan, brown-capped rosy finch) and California (gray-crowned rosy finch), in which regions there is more extensive development of the alpine tundra which remains today in the Southwest.

Boreal Life-zone[26]

The fir forest (Canadian Life-zone) and spruce-alpine fir forest (Hudsonian Life-zone) are frequently considered together as the Boreal Life-zone (boreal forest, Fig. 52), and, in its strictest sense, the Boreal Zone also includes the Arctic-Alpine Zone.

As noted above, the dominant plant life-forms of the Canadian and Hudsonian zones are similar. Also the two zones may merge gradually over wide areas and thus be made difficult to discern because of the partly azonal distribution of the dominant species; this is the problem of the continuum in the ecological distribution of plants and animals. The faunas of these two zones, and the Arctic-Alpine zone as well, are often quite similar in much of the Southwest.

In Arizona in particular there is a considerable intermingling of the vegetation dominants of the Canadian and Hudsonian zones as well as a considerable commonness of faunas, and there is but one species of vertebrate animal (pipit) peculiar to the small area of Arctic-Alpine. Thus it may be more convenient or meaningful for an investigator of some group of animals (vertebrate or invertebrate) to recognize a Boreal Zone; for example, in a biogeographic and evolutionary study of the Boreal Zone mammals of Colorado (Findley and Anderson, 1956).

The elevational range of the Boreal Zone in Arizona inclusive of the alpine tundra is from about 8,000 feet (7,500 feet on north-facing slopes) to 12,670 feet. In Arizona zonal precipitation is approximately 25 to 40 inches annually. Much of it is snowfall in these great western forest watersheds — the reservoirs that feed the permanent springs, streams, and rivers which traverse the arid and semiarid lands far below.

---

[26] Also *Boreal region*. The term *Austral region* was a collective term for Transition, Upper Sonoran or Austral, and Lower Sonoran or Austral; and Tropical region was a third term for "the tropical areas within the United States" and adjacent Latin America (Merriam, 1898:118).

Fig. 52. Boreal Forest. Boreal Life-zone. Spruce, fir, and aspen in the White Mountains. Looking northwest toward Baldy Peak (11,470 ft.) from a camp west of Big Lake, Apache County. The extensive light-colored stand of subclimax aspen in center is on a site of former disturbance (fire) within the forest. It is springtime and the heavy snowpack of winter is lingering on north-facing slopes. Photo by E. Tad Nichols.

SEQUENCE OF THE
BIOTIC COMMUNITIES AND ZONES

From the foregoing discussion of Merriam's Life-zones, it is apparent that, in Arizona, the order of the zones from the lowest elevation (Lower Sonoran) to the highest elevation (Arctic-Alpine) is also the order of decrease in the total geographic area per zone. It may be noted also that Merriam selected names for the zones that are (with the single exception of Transition) quite appropriate in designating a general geographic region in western North America typified by the plant-animal communities represented in the particular zone; that is, the regions where the zones are best developed. When it is further noted that Arizona is closer to Sonora, Mexico than it is to the U.S.-Canadian boundary line, and even farther from the Arctic Circle, it is quite obvious why the extensive area of the two Sonoran Zones alone accounts for over 85 per cent of the total landscape of Arizona, and why the very small area of the Arctic-Alpine Zone is conspicuously less than even the relatively small area of the Canadian and Hudsonian Zones (boreal forest).

The Arctic-Alpine Life-zone occurs at sea level in Alaska and the Lower Sonoran Life-zone occurs at sea level in Mexico. Thus, when going upslope from desert to forest on a high southwestern mountain, one finds a progressive increase in "northern species" of plants and animals some of which extend to the Arctic Circle. Going downslope from forest to desert there is an increase in "southern species" some of which even extend to arid and semiarid lands in South America (see Floral Areas, below). In view of such obvious zonal relationships of life-forms with regard to latitude and "altitude" (elevation), one might expect quite correctly that some more or less valid generalizations have been formulated by biologists, climatologists, *et al.* of both the Old and New World (Humboldt, 1807, 1820; Merriam, 1890; Robbins, 1917; Hopkins, 1918, 1938; Vischer, 1924; Haviland, 1926; Cain, 1944; Good, 1947; Dansereau, 1957; and many others). Merriam discussed the "law of latitudinal equivalent in altitude," noting its early formulation by Alexandre de Humboldt, and he first presented some data and estimates for the Colorado Plateau with special reference to the San Francisco Mountain region in Arizona.

The general proposition, or law of the latitudinal equivalent in elevation, is stated today essentially as it was well over a century ago. That is, that the temperature decrease (lapse) from the equatorial zone to the poles occurs at the average rate (lapse rate) of *ca.* 1° F. for each 1° of latitude; and decreases from a lower to a higher elevation in the same general area at the rate of *ca.* 1° F. for each 330 feet of elevation.

This generalization for the world is made with full cognizance of variations due to regional topography, local influences, and seasonal differences, all of which, of course, affect more than just the temperature gradient. In Arizona the overall (mean annual) thermal lapse rate is close to 4° F. (2.2° C.) per 1000 feet (305 meters) elevation, i.e., approximately 1° F. per 250 ft. (Merriam, 1890; Shreve, 1915; Pearson, 1920, 1930, 1931; Green, 1961). Shreve (1915) found the mean temperature gradient to be 4.1°F. per 1000 ft. on the Santa Catalina Mountains in southern Arizona during 1908-1914. Pearson's data (1920) for 1917 and 1918 show a similar lapse rate of 3.7°F. on a gradient in northern Arizona from desert-grassland at Kingman (3,300 ft.) to timberline (11,500 ft.) on San Francisco Mountain; see Table 3, page 16.

Table 4. Mean Annual Precipitation in Biotic Communities in Arizona and New Mexico. Data from Pearson (1931).

Biotic Community	Inches
Spruce-alpine fir Forest	34
Douglas fir Forest	26
Ponderosa pine Forest	21
Juniper-pinyon Woodland	17
Grassland	11
Desert	10

Temperature inversions result from local disturbing influences that often reverse otherwise linear temperature gradients in mountainous country. It is well known that cold air tends to drain off of high places such as mountain slopes, and to settle in low places such as valleys. Nocturnal downslope cold air drainage causes temperature inversions such as those seen in the reversal in the *minimum* temperature data in Table 3 for the ponderosa pine forest below (colder) and fir forest above (warmer) on San Francisco Mountain; the ponderosa pine zone actually has a shorter frost-free season. Marked temperature inversions are common occurrences in the Rocky Mountain region. Thus milder "thermal belts," of a few hundred vertical feet, often lie between colder air both below and above. It may be surprising but as a general rule, in the Rocky Mountain region, inversions take place during the night at most localities during all seasons of the year.

The greatest distance south to north across Arizona is 392 miles; this is equivalent to 5.68 degrees of latitude. Thus in terms of the law of latitudinal equivalent in elevation and using the relationship for Arizona of 1 degree of latitude per 250 feet elevation, this S-N distance alone may be comparable in its effect on prevailing air temperature to an elevation change of about 1,400 feet. Also, if one assumes the phenological rate of approximately four days equivalence to each 1 degree of latitude in temperate North America (Hopkins, 1918), the spring events in the seasonal biological advance in extreme northern Arizona lag by about 3 weeks those occurring at the same elevation in extreme southern Arizona.

Soil temperature decreases as does the air temperature with elevation. The last killing spring frost is 10-15 days later for each upward 1000 feet, and the frostless season decreases—on the order of 15-30 days per 1000 feet elevation—from the southern desert (40 or more weeks) to forest and tundra (about 15 weeks) according to latitude and locality (Shreve, 1915, 1924; Cannon, 1916; Pearson, 1920; Smith, 1956; Sellers, 1960a).

Elevation ("altitude") is of far greater importance than change in latitude in shaping the character of climate, vegetation, and the resulting biotic communities in Arizona. Coupled with this great variation in height is the remarkably varied topographic variation in space. On elevation

Table 5. Average daily evaporation (E), soil moisture (SM), and the ratio of evaporation to soil moisture (E/SM) for south-facing exposures at six elevations in the Santa Catalina Mountains in southern Arizona during the arid fore-summer of 1911. Data from Shreve (1915).

Habitat	Elevation (Ft.)	Evaporation (E)	Soil Moisture (SM)	E/SM
Forest	8,000	29.3	7.4	3.9
	7,000	62.8	2.6	24.1
Woodland	6,000	59.4	1.8	33.0
	5,000	61.7	3.1	19.9
Desert-Grassland	4,000	80.4	2.0	40.2
Desert	3,000	101.1	2.0	50.5

gradients environmental factors operate together and affect the actual elevational limits of plant and animal species, and hence the sequence of zones and the biotic communities which comprise them. Such major physical factors of the environment in addition to light and soil, are temperature, precipitation, evaporation, humidity, cloudiness, and wind (Tables 3, 4, and 5).

The direction of slope exposure is a powerful indirect factor which causes constant departures of biotic communities from the normal gradient. Just as the lower elevational limit for a species is at a lower elevation on a north-facing slope, so it is that it occurs at still lower elevations on such slopes in the northern part of the state (or its range) than in the southern part. In addition to the steepness of slope and the important effect of slope exposure, the following are some of the often important local influences which interfere with the normal elevational sequence of life-zones (Merriam, 1891; Shreve, 1915; Standley, 1915; Hall and Grinnell, 1919; Jepson, 1925): (1) extent of mountain mass as well as height and base-level (the *Merriam Effect*; Merriam, 1890; Grinnell and Swarth, 1913; Shreve, 1922; Marshall, 1957; Lowe, 1961; Martin, *et al.*, 1961), (2) air currents, (3) cold water streams and drainageways, (4) moist soil evaporation, (5) proximity of large bodies of water, (6) snow banks and glaciers, (7) rock and rocky surfaces, and (8) miscellaneous local influences such as fires and other denuding agents including man, his implements and his domestic animals. All of these influences can in some measure affect a zonal habitat interdigitation that can be seen somewhere on any high mountain in the West. Such downward interfingering of forest and woodland species, however, takes place within narrow canyons and valleys rather than in wide valleys; within wide valleys species of lower zones extend farther upward as they also do on the ridges.

Some of the local influences noted above can produce a *zonal inversion* as can be seen on and directly below the south rim of the Grand Canyon where stands of Douglas fir occur below the pinyons, junipers and ponderosa pines which are on the rim. And even the complete absence of one or more zones may occur in some mountains.

As already noted, the total precipitation (rain and snow) increases while the temperature decreases with increase in elevation. Because of this, the maximum of one factor coincides with the minimum of the other. Consequently, in Arizona the animals and plants with *high moisture* requirements (*e.g.*, spruce trees) must be able to, and do, make a successful living in low temperature environments such as forest or tundra, and those with *high temperature* requirements (*e.g.*, reptiles) must be able to, and do, make a successful living in environments with relatively little moisture, such as desert and grassland. The *upper* elevational range of plant species and animal species on mountains in Arizona is determined by their ability to function at low temperature. The *lower* range limit of woodland and forest species is determined by their ability to resist drought — and for the plants this means the plant-available soil moisture.

The extremes rather than the means of the daily weather elements (and climate) are critical. This is an extension of Liebig's law of the minimum (see Odum, 1959). It is indeed interesting that the upper elevational limits are determined by low temperature and that (1) for forest species, this deficiency of heat manifests itself in *low maximum* temperatures rather than in low minima, while (2) for desert species, *e.g.*, Sonoran Desert, this deficiency of heat manifests itself in the *low minima* of winter (usually in January, Fig. 53). The rapid decrease of physiologic temperature efficiency with increase in elevation (Pearson, 1931) is associated with the remarkably greater frost-hardy adaptedness of the high-elevation genotypes. In Arizona, death from winter-killing by low temperature has relatively little effect on forest (and grassland) species derived from the Arcto-Tertiary Geoflora. However, winter-killing has a very pronounced effect on the tropically related desert species derived from the Madro-Tertiary Geoflora (Shreve, 1911, 1915, 1922; Thornber, 1911; Turnage and Hinckley, 1938; Detling, 1948; Lowe, 1959a). Duration of the temperature in hours or days is often as important a temperature factor as the degree of temperature itself, especially in the case of the extremely low winter minima (Shreve, 1911, 1915).

The average (mean or median) rate of change of precipitation (4-5 inches per 1000 ft.) on typical mountain gradients, or anywhere else in Arizona, is of much less importance than knowledge of the actual variation (extremes) of the rainfall conditions from year to year at a given locality and the effects these have on the plant-available soil moisture. Moisture factors in addition to the precipitation are humidity, cloudiness, wind, evaporation, transpiration (plant), and the all-important resulting soil moisture. Humidity, cloudiness, wind, and temperature are the joint determinants of the rate of evaporation, and evaporation (or evapotranspiration), like temperature, decreases with elevation. The ratio of the evaporation to soil moisture expresses the critical conditions which determine the lower limits of plants on moisture gradients in the Southwest, and these are tremendously different ratios for forest and desert (Table 5). "The ratio of evaporation to soil moisture comprises a measurement of all the external factors which affect the water relations of plants, except the influence of radiant energy on transpiration and the possible effects of soil temperature on this function. It is accordingly unnecessary to give further consideration to rainfall, which is not in itself a factor for vegetation in such a region as Arizona." (Shreve, 1915, page 93.)

Soils in Arizona from desert to forest appear to exert their very important influence on the nature of the biotic community through their physical rather than their chemical characteristics; and by far the most important effect that variation in soils has on all of the biotic communities of Arizona is the direct effect such variation has on the increase or decrease of the plant-available soil moisture. Other things being equal, the more porous soils are best suited for tree growth. In the desert (1) the physical composition of the soil (rock, sand, silt, clay) and (2) its depth are the primary limiting characteristics for both plants and animals. In the forest only the organic content is a major addition to these two characteristics (McGee and Johnson, 1896; Shreve, 1915, 1924, 1951; Pearson, 1920, 1931; Nikiforoff, 1936; Martin and Fletcher, 1943; Marks, 1950; Yang and Lowe, 1956). Desert species reach highest elevations on limestone, next highest on volcanics, and lowest on gneiss (Shreve, 1919).

From the discussions above it is evident that we are particularly indebted to Shreve and to Pearson, as well as to Merriam and others, who were among the early scientific pioneers of environmental gradients on

Fig. 53. Sahuaros (*Cereus giganteus*) killed during extreme freeze of January 12-13, 1962. Paloverde-sahuaro community, 3,200 ft., on rocky slope south side Santa Catalina Mountains. Over 35 per cent of stand in photo was killed; death of up to 70 per cent occurred in some stands. Survivors possess genotypes bestowing greater "cold-resistance." Photo by Richard D. Krizman.

high, rugged mountains in Arizona. They well-documented vegetation gradients on slopes as controlled by environmental moisture and temperature gradients — often steep slopes and gradients from the desert directly up into the forest, with greater environmental change than that between the states of Florida and Maine. In so doing they were documenting the moisture-temperature gradients which control the biotic communities over much of the Southwest. It is significant that Shreve (1915, and elsewhere) working in southern Arizona, and Pearson (1920, and elsewhere) working in northern Arizona arrived at the same conclusions with regard to the correlation of vegetation with the upslope increase in moisture and decrease in temperature and evaporation. That is, as noted above, that (1) the lower elevational limit of a given species of plant on the moisture-temperature gradient is controlled by deficient moisture, and (2) that the upper elevational limit is controlled by deficient heat. It is beyond reasonable doubt that these findings are correct (Daubenmire, 1934a, 1959; Linsey, 1951).

Just as the environmental gradients on mountain slopes are essentially continuous (although variable) linear rates of change, so it is that organisms (plants and animals) are distributed in a more or less continuous type of pattern, *i.e.*, a *continuum* which is more easily seen in the climax pattern of the plants (vegetation) than in that of the animals. Each species of plant and animal, responding on its own to the limits set by its genotype, will "come in" at some point on the gradient and gradually reach its metropolis before finally disappearing at some point still farther along the gradient (Shreve, 1915; Whittaker, 1956, 1960). But a single species of plant sets the limits to the Pacific redwood forest (the coast redwood) just as a single species outlines the ponderosa pine forest (the ponderosa pine), etc. (Mason, 1947).

Such predominant plants and others, and some animals, have been called indicator species, life-zone indicators, etc. (Merriam, 1898; Bailey, 1913; Hall and Grinnell, 1919; Clements, 1920). While "indicators" as such are little discussed any more, they are nevertheless inherent in the thinking and mapping of natural ecologic units such as biome, life-zone, province, type, etc. Witness the boundary between the Great Basin desertscrub and the Southwestern desertscrub *(i.e.*, the northern boundary of the Mohave Desert) drawn on the basis of the northern continental limit (in Nevada and Utah) of but a single species of plant — the creosote-bush, *Larrea divaricata*. And when it is stated that "A subalpine zone begins at about 9,500 feet" in Utah, it is a statement of fact concerning the distribution of but a single species of forest plant, Engelmann spruce (*Picea engelmanni*). Moreover, the entire coniferous forest itself in the Inland Southwest "comes in" on the moisture gradient with the first individuals or stand of the one species of pine (ponderosa) at the lower limit of the ponderosa pine forest; this is ordinarily between 6,000 and 7,000 feet elevation.

Figure 54 depicts the continuum of pines and oaks on southerly exposures on the south-facing side of the Santa Catalina Mountains, "facing" the Sonoran Desert. Note that only one plant (Emory oak) approximates the limits indicated for the evergreen woodland and that no two species of oak have the same span of ecologic tolerance. Note that only one plant (ponderosa pine) approximates the limits indicated for the pine forest and that no two pines· nor trees on the mountain slope coincide in all of their distributional limits. All of these dominant and subdominant species, shown occurring over a vertical distance of 5,000 feet, are in a woodland and forest continuum which begins below as an "open encinal" or oak-grass landscape between 4,000 and 4,500 feet, and increases upslope in density and in cover on the moisture-temperature gradient to an oak-juniper-grass landscape between 4,500 and 5,500 feet, and with increased density, coverage, and floral components to an oak-juniper-pine landscape (oak-pine woodland) that merges with the ponderosa forest above.

The vertical spans of ecological tolerance shown in Figure 54 represent the ecologic summations of the integrated physiological, behavioral, and morphological tolerances of each species. The overlap of these genetically controlled tolerances is the necessity which naturally precedes and permits all of the important biotic relationships which can then be, and are, subsequently established among plants and animals. In the West, and particularly in the desert, the genetic or "individualistic" relation of the plant to environment is far more striking, and more important, than the "organismic" relation of plant to plant. Here the biotic communities that comprise the climax patterns owe their ultimate existence first and decidedly foremost to the coincidental overlap of the genetically controlled spans of tolerance of the comprised species in relation to the environmental gradients and mosaics.

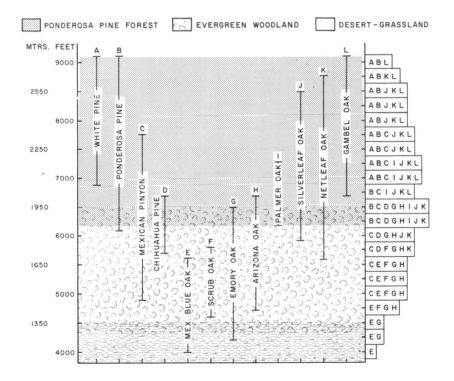

Fig. 54. Amplitudes (spans) of ecologic tolerance for the oaks and pines in the woodland and forest continuum and mosaic on south-facing slopes on the south side of the Santa Catalina Mountains. The overlapping vertical lines indicate the continuum of species frequency distributions; the zipatone background indicates major components of the mosaic. See text.

BIOMES

Some of the American animal-oriented ecologists would prefer to add the term *biome* as an additional label to the major ecologic formations. Thus, for example, instead of speaking of a species that is a forest bird or a grassland bird, one might say a forest biome bird or a grassland biome bird, etc. The term "biome" is redundant. It has most often been used with the purpose of emphasizing the centuries-old and well-known

Table 6. The Ecologic Formations in Arizona and their Equivalent Biome (Shelford) and Life-zone (Merriam) Designations

Ecologic Formations* Lowe, 1961	Biomes* Shelford, 1945	Life-zones Merriam *et al.*, 1910
Desert	. . . .	. . . . .

Southwestern Desertscrub
   (Mohave, Sonoran, and
   Chihuahuan Deserts)
	Creosotebush-Kit Fox
	  (Hot Desert)
		Lower Sonoran

Great Basin Desertscrub
   (Great Basin Desert)
	Shadscale-Kangaroo Rat
	  (Cool Desert)
		Upper Sonoran

Grassland	Gramma Grass-Antelope (Grassland)	Upper Sonoran
Desert-Grassland	. . . . .	" "
Plains Grassland	. . . . .	" "
Chaparral	*Adenostoma*-Brush Rabbit† (Chaparral)	" "
Interior Chaparral	. . . . .	" "
Woodland	. . . . .	" "
Oak Woodland	. . . . .	" "
Pine-oak Woodland	. . . . .	" "
Pinyon-juniper Woodland	Juniper-Rock Squirrel (Pinyon-Juniper Woodland)	
Coniferous Forest	Spruce-Moose† (Coniferous Forest)	Boreal (part)
Pine Forest	. . . . .	Transition
Fir Forest	. . . . .	Canadian
Spruce-fir Forest	. . . . .	Hudsonian
Tundra	*Cladonia*-Caribou†	Arctic-Alpine
Alpine Tundra	. . . . .	"

*Riparian woodland, encinal, and mountain grassland are not listed in the left-hand column of this table; they also lack Shelfordian biome equivalents.

†The names *Adenostoma, Cladonia,* Moose, and Caribou refer to native plants and animals which, of course, do not occur in Arizona, other southwestern states, or in adjacent Mexico.

fact that animals and plants live and function together in natural communities; "biome" is synonymous with ecologic (=biotic) formation and climax (see Table 6) in practice (if not always in theory; see Tansley, 1935). And, as mapped, "biome" is synonymous with climax "plant formation," regardless of the animals present. Thus the major biotic community of associated plants and animals that is the plant-animal formation which we recognize and call *coniferous forest*, has been called the spruce-moose biome, coniferous forest biome, and other "biomes" (see, for example, Shelford, 1932, 1945; Clements and Shelford, 1939; Pitelka, 1941; Allee, *et al.*, 1949; Kendeigh, 1961).

Kendeigh (1948, 1954, 1961) recently has made an interesting attempt to further justify the addition of a still more varied biome terminology to our already somewhat large ecological vocabulary. It may be doubtful, however, that the recognition and study of plant-animal organization, succession and evolution requires the additional ecological jargon (biocies, biociation, biome, biome type, *et al.*). The prior ecological term *formation* (Grisebach, 1838; Weaver and Clements, 1938; and Clements and Shelford, 1939) and its straightforward application in the obvious sense of an ecologic formation (Table 1), *i.e.*, in the only true ecologic sense of a biotic (plant-animal) formation, seems unnecessarily extended to biome, etc.

The paper by Rasmussen (1941) on biotic communities of the Kaibab Plateau in northern Arizona should be consulted. This is a good study carried out under the direction of V. E. Shelford and is found with some surprise to be free of biome jargon. Rasmussen studied both the plants and animals of major biotic communities (forest, woodland, desert) and rejected the frankly annoying implications (of Shelford, Kendeigh, *et al.*) that biome jargon is necessary or even useful for the study and understanding of biotic communities.

BIOTIC PROVINCES

Whereas "life-zones" and "biomes" are fully biogeographic systems, *biotic provinces* are usually, though not always (see Munz and Keck, 1949), more faunistic in their conception. They are continuous geographic areas arbitrarily delimited by various means. Dice (1943: 3) mapped biotic provinces for North America and defined them as follows: "Each biotic province covers a considerable and continuous geographic area and is characterized by the occurrence of one or more important ecologic associations that differ, at least in proportional area covered, from the associations of adjacent provinces."

This definition is, of course, at best a loose one and points to the complexity of criteria often employed, and the obvious subjectivity resulting when they are applied. Vestal (1914) suggested that a biotic province involves similarity in the geographic ranges of animals of ecological similarity, as well as close correspondence between animals and vegetation. Munz and Keck (1949: 88) regard California as a region which "may be divided naturally into a few [5] major biotic provinces, as determined by broad differences in climate." Miller (1951:581) states for biotic provinces, that "Their only essential features seem to be some distinctness of their faunas. Barriers, whether zonal, biotic, or physiographic, are the critical agents that set off an area and its fauna and keep it partly different from that of an adjoining area."

Whatever the criteria employed, and however limited the animal groups emphasized (*e.g.*, small mammals, large mammals, all mammals, or all vertebrates), biotic provinces are concerned with, and usually are intended to show, subcontinental or smaller regions (often quite small) of faunal differentiation (subspecies, species, genera).

By indicating geographic areas of evolutionary differentiation, biotic provinces are not necessarily different from life-zones, biomes, and faunal areas. Biotic provinces are different from life-zones and biomes, however, by being continuous geographic areas, and also by being primarily faunal concepts and representations rather than those of biotic communities. The system may be useful in ecological and evolutionary studies inasmuch as certain regional relationships and differences may be revealed (*e.g.*, Merriam, 1890; Ruthven, 1908; Gates, 1911; Vestal, 1914; Van Dyke, 1919; Dice, 1922, 1939, 1943; Blair, 1940, 1950, 1952; Smith, 1940; Moore, 1945; Goldman and Moore, 1946; Jameson and Flury, 1949; York, 1949; Miller, 1951; Peters, 1955; Denyes, 1956; Munz and Keck, 1959).

Inasmuch as the biotic province was originally a primarily faunistic conception in North America it is not surprising that the more recent as well as early literature on the subject in this country has been largely associated with the investigation of the ecology and distribution of animals rather than plants. Biotic provinces and their uses (and/or misuses) have been discussed recently by Pitleka (1943), Parker (1944), Blair and Hubbell (1938), Allee, *et al.* (1949), Miller (1951), Kendeigh (1954, 1961), Clarke (1954), Woodbury (1954), Peters (1955), Cain and Oliviera Castro (1959), Munz and Keck (1959), and others. The essentials of the concept and its use are well presented most recently by Cain and Oliviera Castro (1959) in their manual of vegetation analysis. Patterns and criteria of distribution in general are recently discussed by Dansereau (1957) and Darlington (1957); see also Hesse, Allee, and Schmidt (1937), Cain (1954), and Beaufort (1951).

C. Hart Merriam (1890) was the first to recognize and name biotic provinces in Arizona. He outlined a "Sonoran province," a "Great Basin province," and a "Boreal province." Dice and Blossom (1937) recognized two biotic provinces in southern Arizona, the "Sonoran province" and "Chihuahuan province." Dice (1939) discussed this further, and named and arranged provinces for Arizona essentially as later mapped (Dice, 1943). These are as follows (Fig. 55; compare with Fig. 1 and Fig. 56):

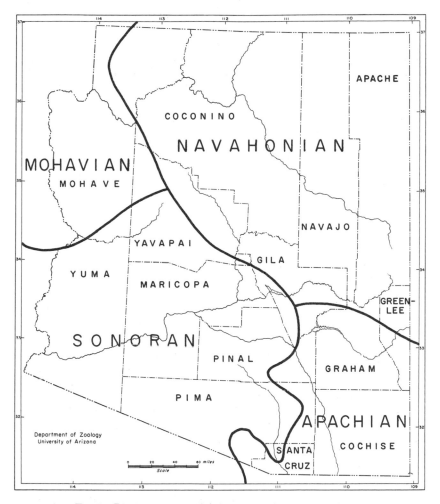

Fig. 55. Biotic provinces of Arizona according to Dice (1943).

1. The *Sonoran biotic province* is desert, and, in Arizona, it is intended to be essentially the area of the state that is within the Sonoran Desert.

2. The *Mohavian biotic province* is essentially the Mohave Desert of other authors (*sensu* Shreve, 1942).

3. The *Apachian biotic province*, according to Dice, is intended to represent the "grassy high plains, and the mountains included in them, of southeastern Arizona, southwestern New Mexico, northeastern Sonora, and northwestern Chihuahua." This is the Yaquian biotic province of others.

4. The *Navahonian biotic province* (Dice, 1943:39), "... is characterized by pinyon-juniper woodland." The "lowest life belt" of the Navahonian is characterized by "arid grassland," and the highest, the "alpine life belt," is made up of treeless areas above timberline. Dice does not mention the Great Basin Desert in his discussion of this province; the southwestern corner of his *Artemisian biotic province* (in the Great Basin) lies in southern Utah.

Dice (1922), Clark (1937), and Davis (1939) have used the term "biotic area," and Allen (1892) used the term "life area," to distinguish smaller plant-animal "units" within a still greater area, say, of the size of the state of Arizona, or of Idaho (Davis, 1939).

FAUNAL AREAS

The essentially, if not purely, faunistic concept and term *faunal area* antedates those of life-zone, biome, and biotic province in North America. Faunal areas are not biotic provinces (in the sense of Dice and Vestal), although they may be similarly conceived and are often equally subjective and difficult to define. Faunal areas may or may not have similar plant associations, but they have dissimilar faunas. Both before and since Allen's use of the term faunal area (1871, 1892, 1893) for the smallest units in his classification and analysis of North American vertebrates (for an area with certain species more or less restricted to it), several investigators have reported on "faunal areas," "faunal districts," etc. of the Southwest (Le Conte, 1859; Cope, 1866, 1875; Packard, 1878; Merriam, 1892; Mearns, 1896, 1907; Townsend, 1897; Brown, 1903; Stevens, 1905; Ruthven, 1907; Grinnell, 1914, 1915; Howell, 1923; Bancroft, 1926; Grinnell, 1928; Law, 1929; Swarth, 1929; Gloyd, 1932, 1937; van Rossem, 1936a; Burt, 1938; Phillips, 1939; Johnson, *et al.*, 1948; Webb, 1950; Miller, 1951; and others; see Law, 1929, for an early critique).

Gloyd (1937) investigated herpetofaunal areas in southern Arizona, mapped them and showed their relationships to the concepts of Mearns (1907) and Swarth (1929). See Figure 56 from Gloyd (1937, Fig. 11) and compare it with Figure 1 (Sellers, 1960b) and Figure 55 (Dice, 1943). Van Rossem (1936a) reached the same general conclusions (based on bird distribution) as those of Gloyd (based on reptile distribution) and further advocated the Baboquivari Mountains rather than the Santa Rita Mountains (Swarth, 1929) as the western boundary of the "Eastern Plains Area."

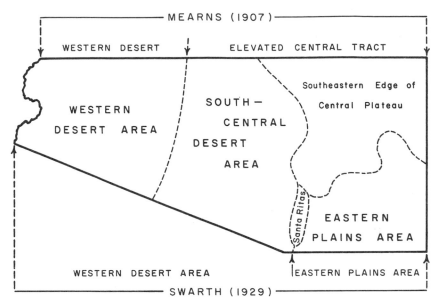

Fig. 56. Faunal areas of southern Arizona, based on the distribution of reptiles, and comparison with the concepts of Mearns (1907) and Swarth (1929); from Gloyd (1937).

Phillips (1939) studied avifaunal areas, reviewed much of the pertinent literature, and recognized four such areas in the state, as follows: "Yuman faunal area," "Pima faunal area," "Mogollon faunal area," and "Navajo faunal area." Phillips and Monson (1936) have also designated "faunal regions" of Arizona based primarily on the geographic distribution of breeding birds.

Faunal areas (faunal districts, faunal territories) are geographic areas or regions where the distributional ranges of several animal species are similar, and where they reach their maximum occurrence. Within the region there are usually a number of the species which are characteristic of other "foreign" faunal areas. Thus a fauna may consist of one or more abstract *faunal elements* such as a Rocky Mountain element, Sierra Madrean, Chihuahuan, Sonoran, Great Basin, Great Plains, Californian, and other elements, which is ordinarily the case for Arizona and other Southwestern "faunas" (see Miller, 1951).

FLORISTIC ELEMENTS

Floras, floristic areas, floristic territories, floristic elements *et al.*, are the plant counterparts in biogeography (floristic geography; see Cain and Castro, 1959). The concept of *floristic element* (=geographic element) as well as of vegetation is important to an understanding of the history and evolution of our present southwestern landscapes (see Axelrod, 1950, 1958).

Arizona and New Mexico, with adjacent parts of Texas and California, sit geographically at the terminus of a host of cool-northern American species which extend this far southward on the continent, and a host of warm-subtropical American species extending this far northward. They meet here and variously co-mingle, in this region called the Southwest, in a complex pattern which is part of a continuum on a subcontinental as well as historical scale. The warm-subtropical species comprise derivative communities of the Madro-Tertiary Geoflora (Southwestern desertscrub, desert-grassland, plains grassland, chaparral, evergreen woodland); the cool-northern species comprise derivative communities of the Arcto-Tertiary Geoflora (alpine tundra, coniferous forest, mountain grassland, Great Basin desertscrub).

This is clearly revealed on a "desert mountain" such as the Santa Catalinas in Arizona. The flora in particular reveals three great segregations of the biota during the Pliocene-Pleistocene into (1) an older *northern* (forest and tundra) element now restricted during the current post-Pleistocene to the higher elevations on the higher mountains, (2) a younger *southern* mixed element at mid-elevations (woodland and chaparral), and (3) our newest, youngest environment existing today — desert — occurring at the lowest surrounding elevations, with its vegetation, flora, and fauna derived through evolution from *southern* subtropical and tropical stocks chiefly during, and since, the Pliocene.

Shreve (1915: 40) discussed the floristic elements in the desert, woodland, and forest vegetation of the Santa Catalina Mountains (to 9,150 feet) in southern Arizona and pointed to several related problems involved in ecology and evolution:

"To summarize for the mountain as a whole, it may be said that the floristic relationships of the Desert and Encinal [Woodland] regions are almost wholly with the Mexican deserts and foothills to the south, while those of the Forest region are divided between the Mexican Cordillera and the Rocky Mountains. The Mexican group is the more conspicuous in the make-up of the vegetation, while the Rocky Mountain contingent is apparently preponderant in number of species."

The following breakdown of the vegetation and floristic elements in the Santa Catalina Mountains is essentially from Shreve (1915).

Desertscrub

The specific and generic relationships of the desert flora (Sonoran Desert) of the Santa Catalinas are, in over 90 per cent of the cases, with Latin America. That is, the relationships are with the Mexican deserts (Sonoran, Chihuahuan, Tehuacan) and semiarid and subtropical lands, the South American deserts and subtropical lands of Argentina and Chile, and to a lesser extent with the Caribbean and Tropical American regions. There is, on the other hand, little relationship with the northerly Mohave Desert and virtually none with the still more northerly Great Basin region, except for some spring annuals. Just the opposite is true for mountain vegetation in *northern* Arizona. Moreover there is relatively little true endemicity (Mogollon element) in the flora of the Santa Catalinas, or, in fact, anywhere in the state.

Grassland

The desert-grassland is of fairly extensive development on all sides of the Santa Catalina Mountains except on the south. On the south side of the mountain the desert-grassland is compressed into a narrow vertical zone of roughly 500 feet elevation on steep gradients at the upper edge of the desert between about 3800-4300 feet elevation where it is confluent with a brief but gradual transition (ecotone) from desert into woodland. The floristic elements are essentially four: Great Plains, Chihuahuan, Sonoran, and Sierra Madrean.

Woodland

The floristic elements in the foothill and mid-elevation evergreen woodland vegetation of the Santa Catalinas are predominantly Madrean; that is, Chihuahuan and Sonoran in the sense of being mid-elevation Sierra Madrean species on both sides of the Cordillera. There is also a Californian element as well as Great Plains, Rocky Mountain, and Eastern North American elements.

Forest

The conspicuous plants in the coniferous forest of the Santa Catalina Mountains (pine forest and fir forest) are primarily Rocky Mountain and Sierra Madrean species. Others represent a Boreal element as well as Californian, Pacific Northwestern, Eastern North American, Mogollon (essentially Arizona-New Mexico), and Cosmopolitan elements.

Shreve (1915:40-41) concluded that:

"It will be impossible to summarize the florlstic relationships of the Santa Catalinas in a thorough manner until very much more is known of their own flora and also of the floras of the many adjacent mountain ranges and desert valleys, both in the United States and Mexico. For the explanation of these relationships a closer acquaintance is needed with the actual mechanisms of transport which are effective in the dispersal of the seeds of desert and mountain plants. *A fuller knowledge is also required of the fluctuations of climate within recent geological time, and of the consequent downward and upward movements of the Encinal and Forest belts of all southwestern mountains* [italics mine]. Such movements would alternately establish and break the connections between the vegetation of the various mountain ranges and elevated plains, thereby permitting the dispersal and subsequent isolation of species which might find no means of movement across the desert valleys under existing conditions."

Shreve wrote this at the former Carnegie Desert Laboratory, on Tumamoc Hill at Tucson. Today Shreve's many far-sighted leads in environmental biology are being enthusiastically followed by several investigators at the University of Arizona where, for example, in the same buildings on Tumamoc Hill, the Geochronology Laboratory of the University is investigating physical, biological, and cultural aspects of arid lands (see "The Last 10,000 years" by Martin, Schoenwetter, and Arms, 1961).

AQUATIC HABITATS

The aquatic fishes and semi-aquatic frogs, turtles, beavers, and other "amphibious" species in Arizona live in either warm-water or cold-water rivers, streams, lakes, or ponds. The major localities in Arizona's warm-water and cold-water fisheries are shown on maps provided in Mulch and Gambel's useful pamphlet (1954) on game fishes in Arizona.

Figure 57 is a drainage map of Arizona (Miller, 1951) which includes those waters supporting permanent populations of native fishes. While there was additional disturbance of some of these waters during the past decade, they remain today largely as shown. The major drainage basins in Arizona are outlined on this map, which also accompanies the check list of fishes (Miller and Lowe, part 2 of this work, 1964).

Figures 58 and 59 show parts of the Colorado River, Arizona's largest, as it courses through the deep gorge that is Grand Canyon. The aquatic fauna of this sizeable Arizona section of the Colorado, which drops 2,000 feet in elevation from *ca.* 3,200 at Lee's Ferry in the Great Basin Desert near the Utah line to *ca.* 1,200 at Hoover Dam (Boulder Dam) in the Mohave Desert in Nevada, is an immensely interesting fauna that has been little studied and is consequently little known.

Figures 65 and 66 are photographs of Aravaipa Creek, a desert stream in the Galiuro Mountains of southern Arizona that is partially canopied by a well-developed riparian woodland climax dominated by cottonwood, willow, and ash (cottonwood-willow gallery association). The desert

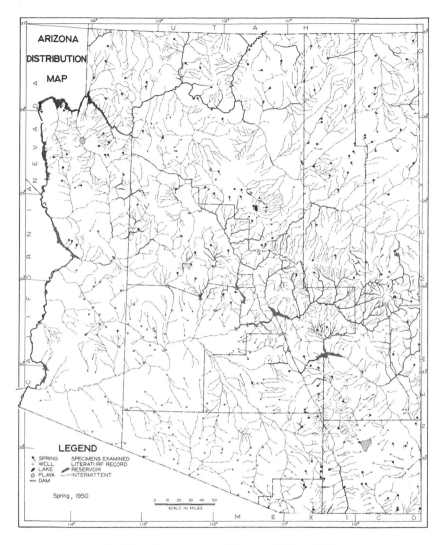

Fig. 57. A drainage map of Arizona (Miller, 1951).

climax here, at 2,600 feet elevation, is paloverde-sahuaro. This fast-flowing, spring-fed stream still supports seven species of native southwestern fishes.[27] These species are now isolated in Aravaipa Creek as remnants of the former and larger fish fauna of San Pedro River (which was formerly a major tributary to Gila River) which is now a dry river bed at the mouth of Aravaipa Creek (north of Mammoth, Pinal County) except at times of flood or run-off.

The high mountain stream habitat of the vanishing Arizona native trout (*Salmo gilae*) is shown in Figure 64.

The ranch pond is a characteristic aquatic habitat in Arizona and is a focal point for vertebrate wildlife. Figure 63 shows a ranch pond (represo, or dirt tank) made of earth, and with a depth of four to five feet. It was successfully planted with the popular bass-bluegill combination at the time the photograph was taken, November 8, 1952. The locality is at 5,000 feet elevation, on the J. A. Jones Ranch in Parker Canyon, south side of the Huachuca Mountains, Cochise County.

The wide variety of Arizona's sport fishing lakes, from the desert near sea level to coniferous forest at over 9,000 feet elevation, are indicated in Figures 59-62. It is of interest that the most widely fished trout in Arizona, rainbow trout (*Salmo gairdneri*), is stocked and taken in each of these lakes where they are associated with cold-water game species in Big Lake in the White Mountains (*ca.* 9,000 feet, Fig. 61), and with warm-water game species in mid-elevation Peña Blanca Lake in southern Arizona near Nogales, Sonora (*ca.* 4,000 feet, Fig. 62), as well as in low-elevation lake Mohave (*ca.* 700 feet, Fig. 60) and other desert area impoundments in the lower Colorado River near sea level.

---

[27] Longfin dace (*Agosia chrysogaster*), spikedace (*Meda fulgida*), Gila sucker (*Pantosteus clarki*), Sonora sucker (*Catostomus insignis*), loach minnow (*Tiaroga cobitis*), Colorado chub (*Gila robusta*), and speckled dace (*Rhinichthys osculus*).

Fig. 58. The Colorado River in Grand Canyon, between Bright Angel Creek and Lake Mead. The shrubby riparian border of mesquite is a characteristic of the banks of the river in the lower part of the gorge, where the Mohave Desert penetrates upstream well into the canyon. Photo by E. Tad Nichols.

Fig. 59. Aerial view of Iceberg Canyon in upper (eastern) end of Lake Mead, on Arizona-Nevada state line. The nearly barren volcanic hills and mountains in this northeastern part of the Mohave Desert support a few scattered shrubs such as brittlebush (*Encelia farinosa*) and occasional clumps of grass such as tanglehead (*Heteropogon contortus*). Photo by E. Tad Nichols.

Fig. 60. Lake Mohave, on Colorado River in Mohave County, is situated in desert-scrub at 650 ft. elevation (Lower Sonoran). It is one of the deep and narrow reservoir lakes in the lower Colorado River which support rainbow trout "all-year-around in the desert," in addition to bass, catfish, panfish, and other warm water species. Photo by Arizona Game and Fish Department.

Fig. 61. Big Lake, in the White Mountains, Apache County, situated in coniferous forest, *ca.* 9,000 ft. (Boreal). Rainbow trout, Arizona's primary stocked trout species, are successfully planted here, as well as in other high mountain lakes, as fry, fingerlings, and catchable-size fish. Photo by Arizona Game and Fish Department.

Fig. 62. Peña Blanca Lake, Santa Cruz County, 3,800 ft.; a mid-elevation lake in an oak-grass landscape near lower edge of evergreen oak woodland. Upper Sonoran. Since filling in 1958, it has been stocked with largemouth bass, black crappie, channel catfish, catchable-size rainbow trout, and threadfin shad as a forage species. Photo by Arizona Game and Fish Department.

Fig. 63. Ranch Pond, oak woodland. Upper Sonoran. J. A. Jones ranch headquarters, 5,000 ft., Parker Canyon, south side Huachuca Mountains, Cochise County. Planted to bass-bluegill combination. Photo by Velma J. Vance, November 3, 1952.

Fig. 64. East Fork of White River, White Mountains, southwest of Baldy Peak, Apache County, May 17, 1950. Boreal. This is the forest stream habitat of the native Arizona trout, *Salmo gilae* Miller. Photo by Robert Rush Miller.

Fig. 65. Riparian Woodland. Lower Sonoran. Aravaipa Creek at 2,600 ft., tributary to San Pedro River (now a dry bed), paloverde-sahuaro foothills, west side Galiuro Mountains, Pinal County. This spring-fed desert stream has a permanent flow of 2-3 feet per second and supports seven species of native fishes (see text). The riparian cottonwood-willow gallery association contains other broadleaf winter-deciduous trees such as sycamore, ash, and walnut.

Fig. 66. Riparian Woodland. Lower Sonoran. Aravaipa Creek at same locality as Figure 65. The *non-riparian climax* of the surrounding desert is typical paloverde-sahuaro on foothills in the Arizona upland section of the Sonoran Desert. The broadleaf trees are the canopy counterpart of a distinctive *climax riparian* community confined here to the desert drainageway.

LITERATURE CITED

Adams, C. C., G. P. Burns, T. L. Hankinson, B. Moore, and N. Taylor
1920a   Plants and animals of Mount Marcy, New York, Part I. Ecology, 1:71-94.
1920b   Plants and animals of Mount Marcy, New York, Part III. Ecology, 1:274-288.

Aldous, A. E., and H. L. Shantz
1924   Types of vegetation in the semiarid portion of the United States and their economic significance. J. Agr. Research, 28:99-128.

Aldrich, J. W. and H. Friedmann
1943   A revision of the ruffed grouse. Condor, 45:85-103.

Alexander, W. H.
1935   The distribution of thunderstorms in the United States. Monthly Weather Rev., 63:157-158.

Allee, W. C.
1926   Some interesting animal communities of northern Utah. Sci. Monthly, 23:481-495.

Allee, W. C., A. E. Emerson, O. Park, T. Park, and K. P. Schmidt
1949   Principles of animal ecology. W. B. Saunders Co., Philadelphia.

Allen, J. A.
1871   On the mammals and winter birds of east Florida with an examination of certain assumed specific characters in birds and a sketch of the bird faunae of Eastern North America. Bull. Mus. Comp. Zool., Harvard College, 2:161-450.
1892   The geographic distribution of North American mammals. Bull. Amer. Mus. Nat. Hist., 4:199-243.
1893   The geographical origin and distribution of North American birds, considered in relation to faunal areas of North America. Auk, 10:97-150.

American Ornithologists' Union Committee
1910   Check list of North American birds. Third edition, New York.

Arnberger, L. P.
1947   Flowering plants and ferns of Walnut Canyon. Plateau, 20:29-36.
1952   Flowers of the Southwest mountains, Southwest Monuments Assoc., Pop. Series, 7:1-112.

Arnold, J. F.
1950   Changes in ponderosa pine bunchgrass ranges in northern Arizona resulting from pine regeneration and grazing. J. Forestry, 48:118-126.

Arnold, J. F. and W. L. Schroeder
1955   Juniper control increases forage production on the Fort Apache Indian Reservation. U. S. Dep. Agr., Rocky Mountain Forest and Range Exp. Sta., Sta. Paper 18:1-35.

Axelrod, D. I.
1950   Evolution of desert vegetation in Western North America. In D. I. Axelrod: Studies in late Tertiary paleobotany. Carnegie Inst. Washington, Publ. 590:1-323.
1958   Evolution of the Madro-Tertiary Geoflora. Botan. Rev., 24:433-509.

Bailey, F. M.
1902   Handbook of birds of the western United States. Houghton Mifflin, Boston, 514 p.
1928   Birds of New Mexico. New Mexico Dept. Game and Fish, Santa Fe.
1939   Among the birds in Grand Canyon Country. U. S. Dept. Interior, Nat. Park Serv., Washington, 211 p.

Bailey, V.
1902   Biological survey of Texas. U. S. Dept. Agr., N. Amer. Fauna, 25:1-222.
1913   Life-zones and crop-zones of New Mexico. U. S. Dept. Agr., N. Amer. Fauna, 35:1-100.
1926   A biological survey of North Dakota. U. S. Dept. Agr., N. Amer. Fauna, 49:1-229.
1929   Life Zones of the Grand Canyon. Grand Canyon Nat. Notes, 3:2-5.
1931   Mammals of New Mexico. U. S. Dept. Agr., N. Amer. Fauna, 53:1-412.
1935   Mammals of the Grand Canyon region. Grand Canyon Nat. Hist. Assoc., Nat. Hist. Bull., 1:1-42.
1936   The mammals and life zones of Oregon. U. S. Dept. Agr., N. Amer. Fauna, 55:1-416.

Baker, F. S.
1945   Forest cover types of western North America. Pamphlet, Soc. Amer. Foresters, p. 1-35.

Baker, W. H.
1956   Plants of Iron Mountain, Rogue River Range, Oregon. Amer. Midl. Nat., 56:1-53.

Ball, E. D., E. R. Tinkham, R. Flock, and C. T. Vorhies
1942   The grasshoppers and other orthoptera of Arizona. Univ. Ariz. Agr. Exp. Sta. Tech. Bull., 93:1-373.

Bancroft, G.
1926   The faunal areas of Baja California del Norte. Condor, 28:209-215.

Bates, C. G.
1924   Forest types in the central Rocky Mountains as affected by climate and soil. U. S. Dep. Agr. Bull., 1233:1-152.

Beaman, J. H.
1962   The timberlines of Iztaccihuatl and Popocatepetl, Mexico. Ecology, 43:377-385.

Beaufort, L. F. de
1951   Zoogeography of the land and inland waters. Sidgwick and Jackson, London.

Benson, L.
1940   The cacti of Arizona. Univ. Ariz. Press, Tucson.

Benson, L. and R. A. Darrow
1944   A manual of southwestern desert trees and shrubs. Univ. Ariz. Biol. Sci. Bull., 6:1-411.
1954   The trees and shrubs of the southwestern deserts. 2nd ed. of Benson and Darrow (1944). Univ. Ariz. Press, Tucson.

Billings, W. D. and L. C. Bliss
1959   An alpine snowbank environment and its effect on vegetation, plant development and productivity. Ecology, 40:388-397.

Blair, W. F.
1940   A contribution to the ecology and faunal relationships of the mammals of the Davis Mountain Region, Southwestern Texas. Univ. Mich. Mus. Zool., Misc. Publ., 46:1-39.
1950   The biotic provinces of Texas. Texas J. Sci., 2:93-117.
1952   Mammals of the Tamaulipan biotic province in Texas. Texas J. Sci., 4:230-250.
1961   Vertebrate speciation. (Editor). Univ. Texas Press, Austin.

Blair, W. F. and T. H. Hubbell
1938   The biotic districts of Oklahoma. Amer. Midl. Nat., 20:425-454.

Blumer, J. C.
1909   On the plant geography of the Chiricahua Mountains. Science, 30: 720-724.
1910   A comparison between two mountain sides. Plant World, 13:134-140.
1911   Change of aspect with altitude. Plant World, 14:236-248.
1912   Notes on the phytogeography of the Arizona desert. Plant World, 15: 183-189.

Brandegee, T. S.
1880   Timberline in the Wasatch Range. Bot. Gaz., 5:125-126.

Brandt, H.
1951   Arizona and its bird life. The Bird Research Foundation, Cleveland, Ohio.

Branscomb, B. L.
1958   Shrub invasion of a southern New Mexico desert grassland range. J. Range Mgmt., 11:129-132.

Bray, W. L.
1905   The vegetation of the sotol country in Texas. Univ. Texas, Bull. 60, Sci. Ser., 6:1-24.

Britton, N. L.
1889   A list of plants collected at Fort Verde and vicinity and in the Mogollon and San Francisco Mountains, Arizona, 1884-1888, by Dr. E. A. Mearns, U.S.A. Trans. New York Acad. Sci., 8:61-76.

Brown, A. E.
1903   The faunal relations of Texas reptiles. Proc. Acad. Nat. Sci., Phila., 55:551-558.

Brown, A. L.
1950   Shrub invasion of southern Arizona desert grassland. J. Range Mgmt., 3:172-177.

Brown, R. J. and J. T. Curtis
1952   The upland conifer-hardwood forests of northern Wisconsin. Ecol. Monog., 22:217-234.

Bryan, K.
1925   The Papago Country, Arizona. A geographic, geologic and hydrologic reconnaissance with a guide to desert watering places. U. S. Geol. Surv. Water Supply Paper 449:1-436.
1928   Change in plant associations by change in ground water level. Ecology, 9:474-478.

Burt, W. H.
1938   Faunal relationships and geographic distribution of mammals in Sonora, Mexico. Univ. Mich. Mus. Zool., Misc. Publ., 39:1-77.

Cain, S. A.
1939   The climax and its complexities. Amer. Midl. Nat., 21:146-181.
1944   Foundations of plant geography. Harper and Brothers, New York.
1950   Life-forms and phytoclimate. Bot. Rev., 16:1-32.

Cain, S. A. and G. M. de Oliviera Castro
1959   Manual of vegetation analysis. Harper and Brothers, New York.

Campbell, R. S. and E. H. Bomberger
1934   The occurrence of *Gutierrezia sarothrae* on *Bouteloua eriopoda* ranges in Southern New Mexico. Ecology, 15:49-61.

Cannon, W. A.
1916   Distribution of the cacti with especial reference to the role played by the root response to soil temperature and soil moisture. Amer. Nat., 50:435-442.

Cary, M.
1911   A biological survey of Colorado. U. S. Dept. Agr., N. Amer. Fauna, 33:1-256.
1917   Life zone investigations in Wyoming. U. S. Dept. Agr., N. Amer. Fauna, 42:1-95.

Castetter, E. F.
1956   The vegetation of New Mexico. New Mexico Quarterly, 26:257-288.

Chaney, R. W., C. Condit, and D. I. Axelrod
1944   Pliocene floras of California and Oregon. Carnegie Inst. Washington, Publ. 553:1-407.

Clark, H. W.
1937   Association types in the north Coast Ranges of California. Ecology, 18:214-230.

Clarke, G. L.
1954   Elements of ecology. John Wiley and Sons, New York.

Clements, F. E.
1920   Plant indicators. Carnegie Inst. Washington, Publ. 290:1-388.

Clements, F. E. and V. E. Shelford
1939   Bio-ecology. John Wiley and Sons, New York.

Cockerell, T. D. A.
1897   Life zones in New Mexico, Pt. I. New Mex. Agr. Exp. Stat. Bull., 24:1-44.
1898   Life zones in New Mexico, Pt. II. New Mex. Agr. Exp. Sta. Bull., 28:137-179.
1900   The lower and middle Sonoran Zones in Arizona and New Mexico. Amer. Nat., 34:285-293.
1941   Observations on plants and animals in northwestern Baja California, Mexico, with descriptions of new bees. Trans. San Diego Soc. Nat. Hist., 9:337-352.

Cockrum, E. L.
1955   Manual of mammalogy. Burgess Publ. Co., Minneapolis.
1963   An annotated check list of the mammals of Arizona. *In* The vertebrates of Arizona. Univ. Ariz. Press, Tucson.

Coleman, B. B., W. C. Muenscher and D. R. Charles
1956   A distributional study of the epiphytic plants of the Olympic Peninsula, Washington. Amer. Midl. Nat., 56:54-87.

Cooke, W. B.
1941   The problem of life-zones on Mount Shasta, California. Madroño, 6:49-55.

Cooper, C. F.
1960   Changes in vegetation structure and growth of southwestern pine forests since white settlement. Ecol. Monog., 30:129-164.

1961a   Controlled burning and watershed condition in the White Mountains of Arizona. J. Forestry, 59:438-442.

1961b   Pattern in ponderosa pine forests. Ecology, 42:493-499.

Cope, E. D.
1866   On the reptilia and batrachia of the Sonoran Provinces of the Nearctic Region. Proc. Acad. Nat. Sci. Phila., 18:300-314.

1875   On the geographical distribution of the vertebrata of the Regnum Nearcticum, with especial reference to the batrachia and reptilia. Bull. U. S. Nat. Mus., 1:55-95.

Cox, C. F.
1933   Alpine plant succession on James Peak, Colorado. Ecol. Monog., 3: 299-372.

Croft, A. R.
1933   Notes on pinyon-juniper reforestation. Grand Canyon Nat. Hist. Notes, 8:151-154.

Cronemiller, F. P.
1942   Chaparral. Madroño, 6:199.

Curtis, J. T. and R. P. McIntosh
1951   An upland forest continuum in the prairie-forest border region of Wisconsin. Ecology, 32:476-496.

Dalquest, W. W.
1948   Mammals of Washington. Univ. Kans. Mus. Nat. Hist., Publ., 2:1-444.

Dansereau, P.
1957   Biogeography, an ecological perspective. The Ronald Press Co., New York.

Darlington, P. J. Jr.
1957   Zoogeography: The geographical distribution of animals. John Wiley and Sons, Inc., New York.

Darrow, R. A.
1944   Arizona range resources and their utilization. I. Cochise County. Univ. Ariz. Agr. Exp. Sta. Tech. Bull., 103:311-366.

1961   Origin and development of the vegetational communities of the Southwest. *In* Bioecology of the arid and semiarid lands of the Southwest. New Mexico Highlands Univ., Bull. 212:30-47.

Darwin, C.
1859   The origin of species by means of natural selection. First Modern Library Edition (1936), New York.

Daubenmire, R. F.
1938   Merriam's life zones of North America. Quart. Rev. Biol., 13:327-332.

1943a   Soil temperature versus drouth as a factor determining lower altitudinal limits of trees in the Rocky Mountains. Botan. Gaz., 105:1-13.

1943b   Vegetational zonation in the Rocky Mountains. Botan. Rev., 9:325-393.

1954   Alpine timberlines in the Americas and their interpretation. Butler Univ. Botan. Studies, 11:119-136.

1959   Plants and environment. A textbook of plant autecology. 2nd ed. John Wiley and Sons, Inc., New York.

Davis, W. B.
1939   The recent mammals of Idaho. Caxton Printers, Caldwell, Idaho.

Deaver, C. F. and H. S. Haskell
1955   Ferns and flowering plants of Havasu Canyon. Plateau, 28:11-23.

Deevey, E.
1949   Biogeography of the Pleistocene. Part I. Europe and North America. Bull. Geol. Soc. Amer., 60:1315-1416.

Dellenbaugh, F. S.
1932   The Painted Desert. Science, 76:437.

Denyes, H. A.
1956   Natural terrestrial communities of Brewster County, Texas, with special reference to the distribution of the mammals. Amer. Midl. Nat., 55: 289-320.

Dessauer, H. C., W. Fox, and F. H. Pough
1962   Starch-gel electrophoresis of transferrins, esterases, and other plasma proteins of hybrids between two subspecies of whiptailed lizard (Genus *Cnemidophorus*). Copeia, 1962 (4) :767-774.

Detling, L. E.
1948   Concentration of environmental extremes as the basis for vegetational areas. Madroño, 9:169-185.

Dice, L. R.
1922   Biotic areas and ecological habitats as units for the statement of animal and plant distribution. Science, 55:335-338.
1939   The Sonoran Biotic Province. Ecology, 20:118-129.
1943   The biotic provinces of North America. Univ. Mich. Press, Ann Arbor.
1952   Natural Communities. Univ. Mich. Press, Ann Arbor.

Dice, L. R. and P. M. Blossom
1937   Studies of mammalian ecology in southwestern North America with special attention to the colors of desert mammals. Carnegie Inst. Washington, Publ. 485:1-129.

Dickerman, R. W.
1954   An ecological survey of the Three-Bar Game Management Unit located near Roosevelt, Arizona. Master's Thesis, University of Arizona, Tucson.

Ditmer, H. J.
1951   Vegetation of the Southwest — past and present. Texas J. Sci., 3:350-355.

Dodge, N. N.
1936   Trees of Grand Canyon National Park. Grand Canyon National Hist. Assoc., Nat. Hist. Bull., 3:1-69.
1938   Amphibians and reptiles of Grand Canyon National Park. Grand Canyon Nat. Hist. Assoc., Nat. Hist. Bull., 9:1-55.
1958   Flowers of the Southwest deserts. Southwestern Monuments Assoc., Pop. Ser., 4:1-112.

Dorf, E.
1960   Climatic changes of the past and present. Amer. Scientist, 48:341-364.

Dorroh, J. H., Jr.
1946   Certain hydrologic and climatic characteristics of the Southwest. Univ. New Mex., Publ. Eng., 1:1-64.

Durrant, S. D.
  1952   Mammals of Utah, taxonomy and distribution. Univ. Kans. Mus. Nat. Hist. Publ., 6:1-549.
  1959   The nature of mammalian species. *In* Species: Modern Concepts. J. Ariz. Acad. Sci., 1:18-21.

Eastwood, A.
  1919   Early spring at the Grand Canyon near El Tovar. Plant World, 22:95-99.

Egler, F. E.
  1951   A commentary on American plant ecology, based on the textbooks of 1947-1949. Ecology, 32:673-695.

Fenneman, N. M.
  1931   Physiography of the western United States. McGraw-Hill Book Co., New York.

Findley, J. S. and S. Anderson
  1956   Zoogeography of the montane mammals of Colorado. J. Mammal., 37: 80-82.

Forsaithe, C. C.
  1920   Anatomical reduction in some alpine plants. Ecology, 1:124-135.

Fosberg, F. R.
  1938   The Lower Sonoran in Utah. Science, 87:39-40.
  1959   Upper limits of vegetation of Mauna Loa, Hawaii. Ecology, 40:144-146.
  1961   Classification of vegetation for general purposes. Trop. Ecol., 1:1-28.

Gardner, J. L.
  1951   Vegetation of the creosotebush area of the Rio Grande Valley in New Mexico. Ecol. Monog., 21:379-403.

Garth, J. S.
  1935   Butterflies of Yosemite National Park. Bull. So. Calif. Acad. Sci., 34: 37-75.
  1950   Butterflies of Grand Canyon National Park. Grand Canyon Nat. Hist. Assoc., Bull. 11:1-52.

Gentry, H. S.
  1942   Rio Mayo plants. A study of the flora and vegetation of the valley of the Rio Mayo, Sonora. Carnegie Inst. Washington, Publ. 527:1-316.

Gleason, H. A.
  1917   The structure and development of the plant association. Bull. Torrey Botan. Club, 44:463-481.
  1926   The individualistic concept of the plant association. Bull. Torrey Botan. Club, 53:7-26.

Glendening, G. E.
  1952   Some quantitative data on the increase of mesquite and cactus on a desert grassland range in southern Arizona. Ecology, 33:319-328.

Gloyd, H. K.
  1932   A consideration of the faunal areas of southern Arizona based on the distribution of amphibians and reptiles. Anat. Record, 54:109-110 (abstract).
  1937   A herpetological consideration of faunal areas in southern Arizona. Bull. Chicago Acad. Sci., 5:79-136.

Goldman, E. A. and R. T. Moore
  1945   The biotic provinces of Mexico. J. Mammal., 26:347-360.

Good, R.
1947   The geography of the flowering plants. Longmans, Green and Co., London.

Gould, F. W.
1951   Grasses of southwestern United States. Univ. Ariz. Biol. Sci. Bull., 7:1-343.

Graham, E. H.
1937   Botanical studies in the Uinta Basin of Utah and Colorado. Ann. Carnegie Mus., 26:1-432.

Grater, R. K.
1937   Check-list of birds of Grand Canyon National Park. Grand Canyon Nat. Hist. Assoc., Nat. Hist. Bull., 8:1-55.

Gray, J.
1961   Early Pleistocene paleoclimatic record from the Sonoran Desert, Arizona. Science, 113:38-39.

Green, C. R.
1962   Arizona climate—Supplement No. 1. Probabilities of temperature occurrence in Arizona and New Mexico. Univ. Ariz. Press, Tucson.

Griggs, R. F.
1934   The edge of the forest in Alaska and the reasons for its position. Ecology, 15:80-96.

1938   Timberlines in the northern Rocky Mountains. Ecology, 19:548-564.

1946   The timberlines of North America and their interpretation. Ecology, 27:275-289.

Grinnell, J.
1908   The biota of the San Bernardino Mountains. Univ. Calif. Publ. Zool., 5:1-170.

1914   An account of the mammals and birds of the Lower Colorado Valley, with especial reference to the distributional problems presented. Univ. Calif. Publ. Zool., 12:1-217.

1915   A distributional list of the birds of California. Pacific Coast Avifauna, 11:1-217.

1928   A distributional summation of the ornithology of Lower California. Univ. Calif. Publ. Zool., 32:1-300.

1935   A revised life-zone map of California. Univ. Calif. Publ. Zool., 40:327-330.

Grinnell, J., J. Dixon, and J. M. Linsdale
1930   Vertebrate natural history of the Lassen Peak region. Univ. Calif. Publ. Zool., 35:1-594.

Grinnell, J. and T. I. Storer
1924   Animal life in Yosemite. Univ. Calif. Press, Berkeley.

Grinnell, J. and H. S. Swarth
1913   An account of the birds and mammals of the San Jacinto area of southern California, with remarks upon the behavior of geographic races on the margins of their habitats. Univ. Calif. Publ. Zool., 10:197-406.

Grisebach, A.
1838   Ueber den Einfluss des Climas auf die Begränzung der natürlichen Floren. Linnaea, 12:159-200.

Hall, E. R.
1946   Mammals of Nevada. Univ. Calif. Press, Berkeley.

118

Hall, H. M. and J. Grinnell
1919   Life-zone indicators in California. Proc. Calif. Acad. Sci., ser. 4, 9:37-67.

Hanson, H. C.
1924   A study of the vegetation of northeastern Arizona. Univ. Nebr. Studies, 24:85-175.

Hargrave, L. L.
1933a   Bird life of the San Francisco Mountains, Arizona. Number One: Summer Birds. Mus. N. Ariz., Mus. Notes, 5:57-60.

1933b   Bird Life of the San Francisco Mountains, Arizona. Number Two: Winter Birds. Mus. N. Ariz., Mus. Notes, 6:27-34.

1936   Bird life of the San Francisco Mountains, Arizona. Number Three: Land birds known to nest in the pine belt. Mus. N. Ariz., Mus. Notes, 9:47-50.

Harshberger, J. W.
1911   Phytogeographic survey of North America. G. E. Stechert, New York.

Hart, F. C.
1937   Precipitation and run-off in relation to altitude in the Rocky Mountain region. J. Forestry, 35:1005-1010.

Haskell, H. S.
1958   Flowering plants in Glenn Canyon. Late summer aspect. Plateau, 31:1-3.

Haskell, H. S., and C. F. Deaver
1955   Plant life-zones. Plateau, 27:21-24.

Hastings, J. R.
1959   Vegetation change and arroyo cutting in southeastern Arizona. J. Ariz. Acad. Sci., 1:60-67.

Haviland, M. D.
1926   Forest, steppe, and tundra. Cambridge Univ. Press, London.

Heald, W. F.
1951   Sky islands of Arizona. Nat. Hist., 60:56-63, 95-96.

Hesse, R., W. C. Allee, and K. P. Schmidt
1937   Ecological animal geography. John Wiley and Sons, New York.

Hoffman, W. J.
1877   The distribution of vegetation in portions of Nevada and Arizona. Amer. Nat., 11:336-343.

Hoffmeister, D. F.
1955   Mammals new to Grand Canyon National Park, Arizona. Plateau, 28:1-7.

Hoffmeister, D. F., and W. W. Goodpaster
1954   The mammals of the Huachuca Mountains, Southeastern Arizona. Ill. Biol. Monog., 24:1-152. Univ. Ill. Press, Urbana.

Holdenreid, R. and H. B. Morlan
1956   A field study of wild mammals and fleas of Santa Fe County, New Mexico. Amer. Midl. Nat., 55:369-381.

Holm, T.
1927   The vegetation of the alpine region of the Rocky Mountains in Colorado. Mem. U. S. Nat. Acad. Sci., 19:1-45.

Holzman, B.
1937   Sources of moisture for precipitation in the United States. U. S. Dept. Agr. Tech. Bull. 589:1-41.

Hopkins, A. D.

1918   Periodical events and natural laws as guides to agricultural research and practice. Monthly Weather Rev., Suppl. 9:1-42.

1938   Bioclimatics. A science of life and climatic relations. U. S. Dept. Agr., Misc. Publ. 280:1-188.

Howell, A. B.

1917   Birds of the islands of the coast of Southern California. Pac. Coast Avifauna, 12:1-127.

1923   Influences of the Southwestern deserts upon the avifauna of California. Auk, 40:584-592.

Howell, A. H.

1921   A biological survey of Alabama: I. Physiography and life-zones: II. Mammals. U. S. Dept. Agr., N. Amer. Fauna, 45:1-88.

1938   Revision of the North American ground squirrels, with a classification of the North American Sciuridae. U. S. Dept. Agr., N. Amer. Fauna, 56:1-226.

Howell, J., Jr.

1941   Piñon and juniper woodlands of the Southwest. J. Forestry, 39:542-545.

Huey, L. M.

1942   A vertebrate faunal survey of the Organ Pipe Cactus National Monument, Arizona. Trans. San Diego Soc. Nat. Hist., 9:355-375.

Humboldt, A.

1807   Essai sur la geographie des plantes. Paris (1805).

Humphrey, R. R.

1949   Fire as a means of controlling velvet mesquite, burroweed and cholla on southern Arizona ranges. J. Range Mgmt., 2:173-182.

1950   Arizona range resources. II. Yavapai County. Univ. Ariz. Agr. Exp. Sta. Bull., 229:1-55.

1953a   Forage production on Arizona ranges. III. Mohave County. Univ. Ariz. Agr. Exp. Sta. Bull., 244:1-79.

1953b   The desert grassland, past and present. J. Range Mgmt., 6:159-164.

1955   Forage production on Arizona ranges. IV. Coconino, Navajo, Apache Counties. A study in range condition. Univ. Ariz. Agr. Exp. Sta. Bull., 266:1-84.

1958   The desert grassland. A history of vegetational change and an analysis of causes. Botan. Rev., 24:193-252.

1960   Forage production on Arizona ranges. V. Pima, Pinal, and Santa Cruz Counties. Univ. Ariz. Agr. Exp. Sta. Bull., 302:1-138.

1962   Range ecology. Ronald Press Co., New York.

Humphrey, R. R. and A. C. Everson

1951   Effect of fire on a mixed grass-shrub range in southern Arizona. J. Range Mgmt., 4:264-266.

Humphrey, R. R., A. L. Brown, and A. C. Everson

1956   Common Arizona range grasses. Univ. Ariz. Agr. Exp. Sta. Bull., 243:1-102.

Humphrey, R. R. and L. A. Mehrhoff

1958   Vegetation changes on a southern Arizona grassland range. Ecology, 39:720-726.

Ingles, L. G.

1947   Mammals of California. Stanford Univ. Press, Stanford.

Ives, J. C.
1861   Report upon the Colorado River of the West. U. S. Senate Ex. Doc., 36th Congress, 1st Session, pt. 1, p. 1-139.

Ives, R. L.
1949   Climate of the Sonoran Desert. Ann. Assoc. Amer. Geog., 34:143-187.

Jameson, D. A., J. A. Williams, and E. W. Wilton
1962   Vegetation and soils of Fishtail Mesa, Arizona. Ecology, 43:403-410.

Jameson, D. L. and A. G. Flury
1949   The reptiles and amphibians of the Sierra Vieja Range of southwestern Texas. Tex. J. Sci., 1:54-79.

Jenks, Randolph
1931   Ornithology of the life-zones. Summit of San Francisco Mountains to bottom of Grand Canyon. Grand Canyon Nat. Park, Tech. Bull., 5:1-31.

Jepson, W. L.
1925   A manual of the flowering plants of California. Univ. Calif. Assoc. Stud. Store, Berkeley.

Johnson, D. H., M. D Bryant, and A. H. Miller
1948   Vertebrate animals of the Providence Mountains area of California. Univ. Calif. Publ. Zool., 48:221-376.

Johnson, I. M.
1919   The flora of the pine belt of the San Antonio Mountains of Southern California. Plant World, 22:71-90, 105-121.

Jones, G. N.
1936   A botanical survey of the Olympic Peninsula, Washington. Univ. Wash. Publ. Biol., 5:1-286.

1938   The flowering plants and ferns of Mount Rainier. Univ. Wash. Publ. Biol., 7:1-142.

Jurwitz, L. R.
1953   Arizona's two-season rainfall pattern. Weatherwise, 6:96-99.

Kearney, T. H. and R. H. Peebles
1942   Flowering plants and ferns of Arizona. U. S. Dept. Agr., Misc. Publ., 423:1-1069.

1951   Arizona Flora. Univ. Calif. Press, Berkeley.

1960   Arizona Flora. 2nd ed. with suppl. by J. T. Howell, Elizabeth McClintock and collaborators. Univ. Calif. Press, Berkeley.

Kendeigh, S. C.
1932   A study of Merriam's temperature laws. Wilson Bull., 44:129-143.

1948   Bird populations and biotic communities in northern lower Michigan. Ecology, 29:101-114.

1954   History and evolution of various concepts of plant and animal communities in North America. Ecology, 35:152-171.

1961   Animal ecology. Prentice-Hall, Inc., Engelwood Cliffs.

Keppel, R. V., J. E. Fletcher, J. L. Gardner, and K. G. Renard
1958   Southwest Watershed Hydrology Studies Group, Tucson. Annual Progress Report, 1958-1960.

Kincer, J. B.
1922   Precipitation and humidity. *In* Atlas of American Agriculture. U. S. Printing Office, Washington, D. C.

1941   Climate and man. U. S. Dept. Agr., Yearbook of Agr.

1946   Our Changing climate. Trans. Amer. Geophys. Union, 27:342-347.

Law, J. E.
1929   A discussion of faunal influences in southern Arizona. Condor, 31: 216-220.

Le Conte, J. L.
1859   The coleoptera of Kansas and eastern New Mexico. Smithsonian Contrib. Knowl., 11:1-58.

Leiberg, J. B., T. F Rixon, and A. Dowell
1904   Forest conditions in the San Francisco Mountains Forest Reserve, Arizona. U. S. Geol. Survey, Prof. Paper 22 (Ser. H, Forestry, 7):1-95.

Leopold, A.
1924   Grass, brush, timber, and fire. J. Forestry, 22:1-10.

Leopold, A. S.
1950   Vegetation zones of Mexico. Ecology, 31:507-518.

Lewis, H.
1959   The nature of plant species. *In* Species: Modern Concepts. J. Ariz. Acad. Sci., 1:3-7.

Lindsey, A. A.
1951   Vegetation and habitats in a southwestern volcanic area. Ecol. Monog., 21:277-253.

Little, E. L.
1941   Alpine flora of San Francisco Mountains, Arizona. Madroño, 6:65-81.
1950   Southwestern trees; a guide to the native species of New Mexico and Arizona. U. S. Dept. Agr., Agri. Handbook 9:1-109.
1953   Check list of native and naturalized trees of the United States (including Alaska). U. S. Dept. Agr., Handbook 41:1-472.

Livingston, B. E. and F. Shreve
1921   The distribution of vegetation in the United States as related to climatic conditions. Carnegie Inst. Washington, Publ. 284: 1-590.

Lloyd F. E.
1907   Pima Canyon and Castle Rock in the Santa Catalina Mountains. Plant World, 10:251-259.

Loew, O.
1875   Report upon mineralogical, agricultural, and chemical conditions observed in portions of Colorado, New Mexico, and Arizona in 1873. U. S. Geog. Surv. W. 100th Merid. (Wheeler), Geol. III, pt. 6, p. 569-661.

Lowe, C. H.
1955   The eastern limit of the Sonoran Desert in the United States with additions to the known herpetofauna of New Mexico. Ecology, 36: 343-345.
1959a   Contemporary biota of the Sonoran Desert: Problems. *In* University of Arizona, Arid Lands Colloquia, 1958-59:54-74.
1959b   Summation—specific and infraspecific variation. *In* Species: Modern Concepts. J. Ariz. Acad. Sci., 1:31-34.
1961   Biotic communities in the sub-Mogollon region of the Inland Southwest. J. Ariz. Acad. Sci., 2:40-49.
1963   An annotated check list of the amphibians and reptiles of Arizona. *In* the Vertebrates of Arizona. Univ. Ariz. Press, Tucson.

Lull, H. W. and L. Ellison
1950   Precipitation in relation to altitude in central Utah. Ecology, 31:479-484.

Lutz, F. E.
1934   From low to high. Grand Canyon Nat. Notes, 9:327-329.

MacDougal, D. T.
1908a   Across Papagueria. Bull. Amer. Geog. Soc., 40:1-21.
1908b   Botanical features of North American deserts. Carnegie Inst. Washington, Publ. 99:1-111.
1921   The reactions of plants to new habitats. Ecology, 2:1-20.

Marks, J. B.
1950   Vegetation and soil relations in the lower Colorado desert. Ecology, 31:176-193.

Marshall, J. T., Jr.
1956   Summer birds on the Rincon Mountains, Saguaro National Monument, Arizona. Condor, 58:81-97.
1957   Birds of the pine-oak woodland in southern Arizona and adjacent Mexico. Pacific Coast Avifauna, 32:1-125.
1962   Land use and native birds of Arizona. J. Ariz. Acad. Sci., 2:75-77.

Martin, P. S.
1959   Terrestrial communities in the Pleistocene. *In* Problems of the Pleistocene epoch and Arctic area. McGill Univ. Mus. Publ. 1:26-38.
1961   Southwestern animal communities in the late Pleistocene. New Mexico Highlands Univ. Bull., Catalog Issue, 1961:56-66.

Martin, P. S. and J. Gray
1962   Pollen analysis and the Cenozoic. Science, 137:103-111.

Martin, P. S., J. Schoenwetter, and B. C. Arms
1961   Southwestern palynology and prehistory. The last 10,000 years. Geochronology Lab., Univ. Ariz. Press, Tucson.

Martin, W. P. and J. E. Fletcher
1943   Vertical zonation of great soil groups on Mt. Graham, Arizona, as correlated with climate, vegetation, and profile characteristics. Univ. Ariz. Agr. Exp. Sta. Tech. Bull. 99:89-153.

Martinez, M.
1945   Las pineaceas mexicanas. Instituto de Biología, México, D.F.
1948   Los pinos mexicanos. Botas, México, D.F.

Maslin, T. P.
1959   The nature of amphibian and reptilian species. *In* Species: Modern Concepts. J. Ariz. Acad. Sci., 1:8-17.

Mason, H. L.
1947   Evolution of certain floristic associations in western North America. Ecol. Monog., 17:203-210.

Mayr, E., E. G. Linsley and R. L. Usinger
1953   Methods and principles of systematic zoology. McGraw-Hill Book Co., New York.

McDonald, J. E.
1956   Variability of precipitation in an arid region; a survey of characteristics for Arizona. Univ. Ariz. Inst. Atmos. Physics, Tech. Rept., 1:1-88.

McDougall, W. B.
1957   Botany of the Museum and Colton Ranch Area. I. General Ecology. Plateau, 29:81-87.

McGee, W. J. and W. D. Johnson
1896 Seriland. Nat. Geog., 7:125-133.

McHenry, D. E.
1932a Demonstration life-zone gardens. Grand Canyon Nat. Notes, 7:81-85.
1932b Quaking aspen at Grand Canyon. Grand Canyon Nat. Notes, 7:87.
1933 Woodland parks on the North Rim. Grand Canyon Nat. Notes, 8: 195-198.
1934 Canadian zone plants on the South Rim of Grand Canyon. Grand Canyon Nat. Notes, 9:301-302.
1935 Quaking aspen—its future in the Park. Grand Canyon Nat. Notes, 9: 361-364.

McKee, B. H.
1933 The naming of the Grand Canyon. Grand Canyon Nat. Notes, 8:210-212.

McKee, E. D.
1934 Flora of Grand Canyon National Monument. Grand Canyon Nat. Notes, 9:310-321.
1941 Distribution of the tassel-eared squirrels. Plateau, 14:12-20.

Mead, P.
1930 A brief ecological comparison of life-zones on the Kaibab Plateau. Grand Canyon Nat. Notes, 5:13-17.

Mearns, E. A.
1896 Preliminary diagnoses of new mammals from the Mexican border of the United States. Proc. U. S. Nat. Mus., 19:137-140.
1907 Mammals of the Mexican boundary of the United States. A descriptive catalogue of the species of mammals occurring in that region; with a general summary of the natural history, and a list of trees. Bull. U. S. Nat. Mus., 56:1-530.

Melton, M. A.
1960 Origin of the drainage and geomorphic history of southeastern Arizona. *In* University of Arizona, Arid Lands Colloquia, 1960-61:8-16.

Merkle, J.
1952 An analysis of a pinyon-juniper community at Grand Canyon, Arizona. Ecology, 33:375-384.

Merriam, C. H.
1890 Results of a biological survey of the San Francisco Mountains region and desert of the Little Colorado in Arizona. U. S. Dept. Agr., N. Amer. Fauna, 3:1-136.
1891 Results of a biological reconnaissance of south-central Idaho. U. S. Dept. Agr., N. Amer. Fauna, 5:1-127.
1892 The geographical distribution of life in North America with special reference to the mammalia. Proc. Biol. Soc. Wash., 7:1-64.
1894 Laws of temperature control of the geographic distribution of terrestrial animals and plants. Nat. Geog. Mag., 6:229-238.
1898 Life-zones and crop-zones of the United States. U. S. Dept. Agr., Div. Biol. Surv., Bull. 10:1-79.
1899a Biological Survey of Mount Shasta. U. S. Dept. Agr., N. Amer. Fauna, 16:1-180.
1899b Zone temperatures. Science, 9:116.

Merriam, C. H., V. Bailey, E. W. Nelson, and E. A. Preble
1910 Zone map of North America. U. S. Dept. Agr., Div. Biol. Surv., Washington, D. C. [This map was used as frontispiece for the third A.O.U. check list of North American Birds, 1910.]

Miller, A. H.
1937 Biotic associations and life zones in relation to the Pleistocene birds of California. Condor, 39:248-252.

1946 Vertebrate inhabitants of the piñon association in the Death Valley region. Ecology, 27:54-60.

1951 An analysis of the distribution of the birds of California. Univ. Calif. Publ. Zool., 50:531-643.

Miller, F. H.
1921 Reclamation of grasslands by Utah juniper on the Tusayan National Forest, Arizona. J. Forestry, 19:647-651.

Miller, G. S.
1895 The long-tailed shrews of the eastern United States. U. S. Dept. Agr., N. Amer. Fauna, 10:35-56.

1897 Revision of the North American bats of the family Vespertilionidae. U. S. Dept. Agr., N. Amer. Fauna, 13:1-135.

Miller, R. R.
1954 A drainage map of Arizona. Syst. Zool., 3:80-81.

Miller, R. R. and C. H. Lowe
1963 An annotated check list of the fishes of Arizona. *In* Vertebrates of Arizona. Univ. Ariz. Press, Tucson.

Monson, G.
1942 Notes on some birds of southeastern Arizona. Condor, 44:222-225.

Monson, G. and A. R. Phillips
1941 Bird records from southern and western Arizona. Condor, 43:108-112.

Moore, R. T.
1945 The transverse volcanic biotic province of central Mexico and its relationship to adjacent provinces. Trans. San Diego Soc. Nat. Hist., 10: 217-235.

Muesebeck, C. F. W. and K. V. Krombein
1952 Life-zone map. Syst. Zool., 1:24-25.

Mulch, E. E. and W. C. Gamble
1954 Game fishes of Arizona. Ariz. Game and Fish Dept.

Muller, C. H.
1939 Relations of the vegetation and climatic types in Nuevo Leon, Mexico. Amer. Midl. Nat., 21:687-729.

1940 Plant succession in the *Larrea-Flourensia* climax. Ecology, 21:206-212.

Munns, E. N.
1938 The distribution of important forest trees of the United States. U. S. Dept. Agr., Misc. Publ., 287:1-176.

Munz, P. A. and D. D. Keck
1949 California plant communities. El Aliso, 2:87-105, 199-202.

1959 A California flora. Univ. Calif. Press, Berkeley.

Murie, O. J.
1951 The elk of North America. Wildlife Mgmt. Inst., Washington, D. C.

Murray, A. V.
1959 An analysis of changes in Sonoran Desert vegetation for the years 1928-1957. Master's thesis, The University of Arizona, Tucson.

Nelson, E. W.
1922   Lower California and its natural resources. Mem. [U. S.] Nat. Acad. Sci., 16: 1-194.

Nichol, A. A.
1937   The natural vegetation of Arizona. Univ. Ariz. Agr. Exp. Sta. Tech. Bull., 68:181-222. 2nd ed., 1952, Tech. Bull., 127:189-230.

Nikiforoff, C. C.
1937   General trends of the desert type of soil formation. Soil Sci., 43: 105-131.

Norris, J. J.
1950   Effect of rodents, rabbits, and cattle on two vegetation types in semi-desert range land. New Mexico Agr. Exp. Sta. Bull. 353:1-24.

Norris, K. S.
1958   The evolution and systematics of the iguanid genus *Uma* and its relation to the evolution of other North American reptiles. Bull. Amer. Mus. Nat. Hist., 114:251-326.

Odum, E. P.
1945   The concept of the biome as applied to the distribution of North American birds. Wilson Bull., 57:191-201.
1959   Fundamentals of ecology. 2nd ed. W. B. Saunders Co., Philadelphia.

Olin, G.
1959   Mammals of the southwest deserts. 2nd ed. Southwestern Monuments Assoc., Pop. Ser., 8:1-112.
1961   Mammals of the southwest mountains and mesas. Southwestern Monuments Assoc., Pop. Ser., 9:1-126.

Osgood, W. H.
1900   Revision of the pocket mice of the genus Perognathus. U. S. Dept. Agr., N. Amer. Fauna, 18:1-73.

Packard, A. S. Jr.
1878   Some characteristics of the central zoo-geographical province of the United States. Amer. Nat., 12:512-517.

Parker, D.
1944   Review of Dice's "Biotic provinces of North America." Amer. Midl. Nat., 32:254.

Parker, K. W.
1945   Juniper comes to the grasslands: why it invades southwestern grassland — suggestions on control. Amer. Cattle Producer, 27:12-14, 30-32.

Parker, K. W. and S. C. Martin
1952   The mesquite problem on southern Arizona ranges. U. S. Dept. Agr. Circ. 908:1-70.

Patraw, P. M.
1931   Plant succession on Kaibab limestone. Grand Canyon Nat. Notes, 6:6-9.
1953   Flowers of the southwest mesas. Southwestern Monuments Assoc., Pop Ser., 5:1-112.

Pearson, G. A.
1920a   Factors controlling the distribution of forest types, Part I. Ecology, 1:139-159.
1920b   Factors controlling the distribution of forest types, Part II. Ecology, 1:289-308.

Pearson, G. A.

1930   Studies of climate and soil in relation to forest management in the Southwestern United States. Ecology, 18:139-144.

1931   Forest types in the Southwest as determined by climate and soil. U. S. Dept. Agr. Tech. Bull. 247:1-144.

1933   The conifers of northern Arizona. Plateau, 6:1-7.

1942   Herbaceous vegetation a factor in natural regeneration of ponderosa pine in the Southwest. Ecol. Monog., 12:315-338.

1950   Management of ponderosa pine in the Southwest. U. S. Dept. Agr., Forest Serv. Monog. 6:1-218.

Peattie, D. C.

1953   A natural history of western trees. Houghton-Mifflin, Boston.

Peters, J. A.

1955   Use and misuse of the biotic province concept. Amer. Nat., 89:21-28.

Peterson, R. T.

1941   A field guide to western birds. Houghton-Mifflin, Boston.

1942   Life-zones, biomes, or life-forms? Audubon Mag., 44:21-30.

Phillips, A. R.

1939   The faunal areas of Arizona, based on bird distribution. Master's thesis, The University of Arizona.

1956   The migrations of birds in Northern Arizona. Plateau, 29:31-35.

1959   The nature of avain species. *In* Species: Modern concepts. J. Ariz. Acad. Sci., 1:22-30.

Phillips, A. R. and G. Monson

1963   An annotated check list of the birds of Arizona. *In* The Vertebrates of Arizona. Univ. Ariz. Press, Tucson.

Pitelka, F. A.

1941   Distribution of birds in relation to major biotic communities. Amer. Midl. Nat., 25:113-137.

1943   Review of Dice's "Biotic Provinces of North America." Condor, 45:203-204.

Preble, E. A.

1923   A biological survey of the Pribilof Islands, Alaska. Life-zone relationships. U.S. Dept. Agr., N. Amer. Fauna, 46:1-255.

Preston, R. J., Jr.

1947   Rocky Mountain trees. 2nd ed., Ames, Iowa.

Rasmussen, D. I.

1941   Biotic communities of Kaibab Plateau, Arizona. Ecol. Monog., 11:229-275.

Raup, H. M.

1951   Vegetation and cryoplanation. Ohio J. Sci., 51:105-116.

Read, A. D.

1915   The flora of the Williams Division of the Tusayan National Forest, Arizona. Plant World, 18:112-123.

Reed, T. A.

1933   The North American high-level anticyclone. Monthly Weather Rev., 61:321-325.

1939   Thermal aspects of the high-level anticyclone. Monthly Weather Rev., 67.

Reynolds, H. G. and J. W. Bohning

1956   Effects of burning on a desert grass-shrub range in southern Arizona. Ecology, 37:769-777.

Robbins, W. W.

1917   Native vegetation and climate of Colorado in their relation to agriculture. Colorado Agr. Exp. Sta. Bull. 224:1-56.

Robinson, H. H

1913   The San Franciscan volcanic field, Arizona. U. S. Geol. Surv. Prof. Paper 76:1-213.

Rusby, H. H.

1889   General floral features of the San Francisco and Mogollon Mountains of Arizona and New Mexico, and their adjacent regions. Trans. N. Y. Acad. Sci., 8:76-81.

Ruthven, A. G.

1907   A collection of reptiles and amphibians from southern New Mexico and Arizona. Bull. Amer. Mus. Nat. Hist., 23:483-604.

1908   The faunal affinities of the prairie region of central North America. Amer. Nat., 42:388-393.

Rydberg, P. A.

1914   Phytogeographical notes on the Rocky Mountain region. II. Origin of the alpine flora. Bull. Torrey Botan. Club, 41:89-103.

1916   Vegetative life-zones of the Rocky Mountain Region. Mem. N. Y. Bot. Garden, 6:477-499.

Rzedowski, J.

1956   Notas sobre la flora y la vegetación del estado de San Luis Potosí. III. Vegetación de la región de Guadalcazar. Anales del Instituto de Biología, México, D.F., 27:169-228.

Sampson, A. W.

1918   Climate and plant growth in certain vegetative associations. Bull. U. S. Dept. Agr., 700:1-72.

Sargent, C. S.

1926   Manual of the trees of North America (exclusive of Mexico). 2nd ed., Boston.

Saunders, A. A.

1921   A distributional list of the birds of Montana. Pac. Coast Avifauna, 14: 1-194.

Schroeder, W. L.

1953   History of juniper control on the Fort Apache Reservation. Ariz. Cattle-log, 8:18-25.

Schulman, E.

1956   Dendroclimatic changes in semiarid America. Univ. Ariz. Press, Tucson.

Schwalen, H. C.

1942   Rainfall and runoff in the upper Santa Cruz River drainage basin. Univ. Ariz. Agr. Exp. Sta. Tech. Bull. 95:421-472.

Sclater, P. L.

1858   On the general geographic distribution of the members of the class Aves. J. of Proc. Linnaean Soc. London (Zool.), 2:130-145.

Sellers, W. D.

1960a   Arizona Climate. (Editor) Univ. Ariz. Press, Tucson.

1960b   The climate of Arizona. *In* Arizona Climate, Univ. Ariz. Press, Tucson.

Shantz, H. L.

1936   Vegetation. *In* Arizona and its heritage. Univ. Ariz., Gen. Bull. 3:46-52.

Shantz, H. L. and R. L. Piemeisel

1925   Indicator significance of the natural vegetation of the southwestern desert region. J. Agr. Res., 28:721-801.

Shantz, H. L. and R. Zon
1924   Natural vegetation. U. S. Dept. Agr., Atlas of Amer. Agr., pt. 1, sec. E. Washington.

Shaw, C. H.
1909   The causes of timber line on mountains; the role of snow. Plant World, 12:169-181.

Shelford, V. E.
1932   Life-zones, modern ecology, and the failure of temperature summing. Wilson Bull., 44:144-157.
1945   The relative merits of the life zone and biome concepts. Wilson Bull., 57:248-252.

Shreve, F.
1911   The influence of low temperature on the distribution of the giant cactus. Plant World, 14:136-146.
1914   A montane rain-forest. A contribution to the physiological plant geography of Jamaica. Carnegie Inst. Washington, Publ. 199:1-110.
1915   The vegetation of a desert mountain range as conditioned by climatic factors. Carnegie Inst. Washington, Publ. 217:1-112.
1917a   The physical control of vegetation in rain-forest and desert mountain. Plant World, 20:135-141.
1917b   A map of the vegetation of the United States. Geog. Rev., 3:119-125.
1919   A comparison of the vegetational features of two desert mountain ranges. Plant World, 22:291-307.
1922   Conditions indirectly affecting vertical distribution on desert mountains. Ecology, 3:269-274.
1924   Soil temperature as influenced by altitude and slope exposure. Ecology, 5:128-136.
1925   Ecological aspects of the deserts of California. Ecology, 6:93-103.
1929   Changes in desert vegetation. Ecology, 10:364-373.
1934   Vegetation of the northwestern coast of Mexico. Bull. Torrey Botan. Club, 61:373-380.
1936   The plant life of the Sonora Desert. Sci. Monthly, 42:195-213.
1939   Observations on the vegetation of Chihuahua. Madrono, 5:1-13.
1942a   The vegetation of Arizona. *In* Flowering plants and ferns of Arizona, by T. H. Kearney and R. H. Peebles. U. S. Dept. Agr. Misc. Publ., 423:10-23.
1942b   The desert vegetation of North America. Botan. Rev., 8:195-246.
1942c   Grassland and related vegetation in northern Mexico. Madroño, 6:190-198.
1944   Rainfall of northern Mexico. Ecology, 25:105-111.
1951   Vegetation and flora of the Sonoran Desert. Vol. I, Vegetation. Carnegie Inst. Washington, Publ. 591:1-192.

Shreve, F. and A. L. Hinckley
1937   Thirty years of change in desert vegetation. Ecology, 18:463-478.

Smith, A. P.
1908   Some data and records from the Whetstone Mountains, Arizona. Condor, 10:75-78.

Smith, H. M.
1940   An analysis of the biotic provinces of Mexico, as indicated by the distribution of the lizards of the genus *Sceloporus*. Anales Escuela Nac. Ciencias Biol., Mexico, 1:96-110.

Smith, H. V.
1956   The climate of Arizona. Univ. Ariz. Agr. Exp. Sta. Bull. 279:1-99.

Soper, J. D.

1946   Mammals of the northern Great Plains along the international boundary in Canada. J. Mammal., 27:127-153.

Spaulding, V. M.

1909   Distribution and movements of desert plants. Carnegie Inst. Washington, Publ. 113:1-144.

1910   Plant associations of the Desert Laboratory domain and adjacent valley. Plant World, 13:31-42.

Spangle, P. and M. Sutton

1949   The botany of Montezuma Well. Plateau, 22:11-19.

Standley, P. C.

1915   Vegetation of the Brazos Canyon, New Mexico. Plant World, 18:179-191.

Stebbins, R. C.

1949   Speciation in salamanders of the plethodontid genus *Ensatina*. Univ. Calif. Publ. Zool., 48:377-526.

1954   Amphibians and reptiles of Western North America. McGraw-Hill Book Co., New York.

Stejneger, L.

1893   Annotated list of the reptiles and batrachians collected by the Death Valley Expedition in 1891, with descriptions of new species. *In* U. S. Dept. Agr., N. Amer. Fauna, 7:159-228.

Stevens, J. S.

1905   Life areas of California. Trans. San Diego Soc. Nat. Hist., 1:1-25.

Storer, T. I. and R. L. Usinger

1957   General Zoology. McGraw-Hill Book Co., New York.

Sturdevant, G. E.

1927   Flora of the Tonto Platform. Grand Canyon Nat. Notes, 1:1-2.

Sudworth, G. B.

1915   The cypress and juniper trees of the Rocky Mountain region. U. S. Dept. Agr. Bull., 207:1-36.

1934   Poplars, principal tree willows and walnuts of the Rocky Mountain region. U. S. Dept. Agr. Bull., 680:1-45.

Sutton, M.

1952   A botanical reconnaissance in Oak Creek Canyon. Plateau, 25:30-42.

Sutton, G. M. and A. R. Phillips

1942   June bird life of the Papago Indian Reservation, Arizona. Condor, 44:57-65.

Swarth, H. S.

1914   A distributional list of the birds of Arizona. Pac. Coast Avifauna, 10:1-133.

1920   Birds of the Papago Saguaro National Monument and the neighboring region, Arizona. U. S. Dept. Interior, National Park Service. 63 p.

1929   Faunal areas of southern Arizona; a study in animal distribution. Proc. Calif. Acad. Sci., 18:267-383.

Sykes, G.

1931   Rainfall investigation in Arizona and Sonora by means of long-period rain gauges. Geog. Rev., 21:229-233.

Tansley, A. G.

1935   The use and abuse of vegetational concepts and terms. Ecology, 16:284-307.

Taylor, W. P.
1922   A distributional and ecological study of Mt. Ranier, Washington. Ecology, 3:214-236.

Thornber, J. J.
1910   The grazing ranges of Arizona. Univ. Ariz. Agr. Exp. Sta. Bull., 65: 245-360.
1911   Plant acclimatization in southern Arizona. Plant World, 14:15-23.

Townsend, C. H. T.
1893   On the life zones of the Organ Mountains and adjacent region in southern New Mexico, with notes on the fauna of the range. Science, 22: 313-315.
1895-97 On the bio-geography of Mexico, Texas, New Mexico, and Arizona, with special reference to the limits of the life areas, and a provisional synopsis of the bio-geographic divisions of America. Trans. Texas Acad. Sci., 1 (1895):71-96; 2 (1897):33-86.

Turnage, W. V. and H. L. Hinkley
1938   Freezing weather in relation to plant distribution in the Sonoran Desert. Ecol. Monog., 8:529-550.

Turnage, W. V. and T. D. Mallory
1941   An analysis of rainfall in the Sonoran Desert and adjacent territory. Carnegie Inst. Washington, Publ. 529:1-110.

Turner, R. M.
1959   Evolution of the vegetation of the southwestern desert region. *In* University of Arizona, Arid Lands Colloquia, 1958-59:46-53.

U. S. Forest Service
1949   Areas characterized by major forest types in the United States (map). U. S. Dept. Agr. Washington, D. C.

van Rossem, A. J.
1931   Report on a collection of land· birds from Sonora, Mexico. Trans. San Diego Soc. Nat. Hist., 6:237-304.
1932   The avifauna of Tiburon Island, Sonora, Mexico, with descriptions of four new races. Trans. San Diego Soc. Nat. Hist., 7:119-150.
1936a   Notes on birds in relation to the faunal areas of south-central Arizona. Trans. San Diego Soc. Nat. Hist., 8:122-148.
1936b   Birds of the Charleston Mountains, Nevada. Pac. Coast Avifauna, 24: 1-65.
1945   A distributional survey of the birds of Sonora, Mexico. Louisiana State Univ. Mus. Zool., Occ. Paper, 21:1-379.

Van Tyne, J. and A. J. Berger
1959   Fundamentals of ornithology. John Wiley and Sons, Inc., New York.

Vestal, A. G.
1914   Internal relations of terrestrial associations. Amer. Nat., 48:413-445.

Visher, S. S.
1924   Climatic laws. Ninety generalizations with numerous corollaries as to the geographic distribution of temperature, wind, moisture, etc. A summary of climate. John Wiley and Sons, Inc., New York.

Vorhies, C. T., R. Jenks and A. R. Phillips
1935   Bird records from the Tucson region, Arizona. Condor, 37:243-247.

Wallace, A. R.
1876   The geographical distribution of animals, with a study of the relations of living and extinct faunas as elucidating the past changes of the earth's surface. MacMillan and Co., London.

Wallmo, O. C.

1955 Vegetation of the Huachuca Mountains, Arizona. Amer. Midl. Nat., 54:466-480.

Weaver, J. E. and F. E. Clements

1938 Plant ecology. McGraw-Hill Book Co., New York.

Webb, W. L.

1950 Biogeographic regions of Texas and Oklahoma. Ecology, 31:426-433.

Webster, G. L.

1961 The altitudinal limits of vascular plants. Ecology, 42:587-590.

Whitfield, C. J. and E. L. Beutner

1938 Natural vegetation in the desert plains grassland. Ecology, 19:26-37.

Whitfield, C. J. and H. L. Anderson

1938 Secondary succession in the desert plains grassland. Ecology, 19:171-180.

Whittaker, R. H.

1951 A criticism of the plant association and climatic climax concepts. Northwest Sci., 25:17-31.

1953 A consideration of climax theory: The climax as a population and pattern. Ecol. Monog., 23:41-78.

1956 Vegetation of the Great Smoky Mountains. Ecol. Monog., 26:1-80.

1957 Recent evolution of ecological concepts in relation to the eastern forests of North America. Amer. J. Botan., 44:197-206.

1960 Vegetation of the Siskiyou Mountains, Oregon and California. Ecol. Monog., 30:275-338.

Willet, G.

1933 A revised list of the birds of southwestern California. Pac. Coast Avifauna, 21:1-204.

Woodbury, A. M.

1947 Distribution of pigmy conifers in Utah and northeastern Arizona. Ecology, 28:113-126.

1954 Principles of general ecology. The Blakiston Co., New York.

Woodbury, A. M. and H. N. Russell, Jr.

1945 Birds of the Navajo Country. Univ. Utah Bull. 35, Biol. Ser. 9(1): 1-160.

Woodin, H. E. and A. A. Lindsey

1954 Juniper-piñon east of continental divide, as analyzed by the line-strip method. Ecology, 35:473-489.

Woolsey, T. S.

1911 Western yellow pine in Arizona and New Mexico. U. S. Dept. Agr. Forest Serv. Bull., 101:1-33.

Wooton, E. O. and P. C. Standley

1913 Description of new plants, preliminary to a report on the flora of New Mexico. Contrib. U. S. Nat. Herbarium, 16:109-196.

Yang, T. W.

1957 Vegetational, edaphic, and faunal correlations of the western slope of the Tucson Mountains and the adjoining Avra Valley. Ph.D. Dissertation, The University of Arizona.

1961 The recent expansion of creosotebush (*Larrea divaricata*) in the North American desert. Western Reserve Academy, Nat. Hist. Mus., 1:-1-11.

Yang, T. W. and C. H. Lowe
  1956   Correlation of major vegetation climaxes with soil characteristics in the Sonoran Desert. Science, 123:542.

York, C. L.
  1949   The physical and vegetational basis for animal distribution in the Sierra Vieja Range of southwestern Texas. Tex. J. Sci., 3:46-62.

Zweifel, R. S.
  1962   Analysis of hybridization between two subspecies of the desert whiptailed lizard, *Cnemidophorus tigris*. Copeia, 1962 (4) :749-766.

INDEX